Puppy
Care and Training

An Owner's Guide To

A HAPPY HEALTHY PET

Howell Book House

Howell Book House
A Simon & Schuster Macmillan Company
1633 Broadway
New York, NY 10019

MACMILLAN is a registered trademark of Macmillan, Inc.

Library of Congress Cataloging-in-Publication Data
McLennan, Bardi,
Puppy care and training/Bardi McLennan.
ISBN: 0-8765-391-6
1. Puppies. 2. Puppies—Training. I. Title.
SF427.M4735   1996
636.7'07—dc20   95-41345
            CIP

Manufactured in the United States of America
10 9

Series Director: Dominique De Vito
Series Assistant Director: Ariel Cannon
Book Design: Michele Laseau
Cover Design: Iris Jeromnimon
Illustration: Jeff Yesh
Photography:
  Cover: Pets by Paulette; Back Cover: Jean Wentworth
  Joan Balzarini: 40, 47, 120
  Mary Bloom: 73
  Paulette Braun/Pets by Paulette: 5, 9, 26, 30, 42, 44, 55, 57, 61, 70, 77, 88, 103
  Judith Strom: 4, 6, 7, 11, 12, 13, 18, 21, 24–25, 29, 31, 32, 36, 37, 39, 48, 50, 52, 53,
    56, 58, 59, 60, 62, 63, 64, 72, 76, 78, 79, 82, 89, 91, 93, 94, 95, 96, 102, 122, 129,
    131, 150
  Jean Wentworth: 2–3, 14, 17, 20, 34, 35, 67, 80, 100–101, 114, 121, 125
  Kerrin Winter/Dale Churchill: 81, 84, 85, 87, 98
Production Team: Trudy Brown, Jama Carter, Kathleen Caulfield, Trudy Coler,
  Amy DeAngelis, Pete Fornatale, Matt Hannafin, Kathy Iwasaki, Vic Peterson,
  Terri Sheehan, Marvin Van Tiem, and Kathleen Varanese

Contents

Welcoming a

part one

Puppy

Congratulations
on Your New
Puppy!

Puppies bring with them all kinds of things, some of which are the very reasons you chose the pup you did—playful exuberance, a sweet face, a soft warm body to cuddle, and charm. Puppies not only arrive in their new homes with an abundance of charm, they all seem to come into the world knowing exactly how to use it to beguile their new owners. In fact, being taken in by your puppy's charisma may just be what marks

(Afghan Hound)

the start of a lifelong friendship. The memories of naughtiness fade, but the charm remains.

Puppies also come "complete with batteries." Everything is already in place for a puppy to absorb its environment like a sponge. The pup learns from every gesture of your arms, legs, face; from your tone of voice; from how you speak to others and how differently you speak to him. Your puppy has an inner clock that quickly resets to his new household's routine—when to wake up, when to eat, when Johnny leaves for school, when to go to sleep. Everything. And he learns it all in a matter of days!

What you teach, *how* you teach and *when* you teach will determine what kind of adult your puppy becomes. If everyone in the household races to answer the phone, one ding-a-ling will be the starter's gun for the puppy, too. On the other hand, you can (and should) teach your puppy to sit-stay when you are on the phone.

Note the use of "teach" rather than "train." Teaching allows your puppy to participate in the learning process. You teach and the pup learns. Training is essentially robotic. Soldiers are trained. Circus animals are trained. It's the "don't think, just obey" method and it should not be used on puppies. A year from now, if you're considering competitive obedience, you may decide to go that route, which is okay because by then your puppy will have *learned* how to understand instructions.

The puppy has so much to learn that he may become sloppy about house rules only because he is in such a hurry to know it all. It is your responsibility (in addition to basic care) to maintain consistency in disciplining the puppy. Discipline in this case is positive *teaching*, not punishment. Each person in the family needs to know and to use the same "action" words (sit, come, off, etc.) in the same tone of voice, requiring the same outcome in order not to confuse the puppy. It is truly not complicated—we'll go into it in detail.

Preparing for Your Puppy

There are a few things that should have been taken care of before you brought the puppy home, but it's not too late to do them *today!*

First is to locate a veterinarian (your pup's second-best friend). You can often get a referral from your pup's breeder, or from friends, relatives or neighbors who take good care of their dogs. Call to make a get-acquainted appointment. In some areas, vets are overloaded and can't take on new patients, and you may have to ask for yet another referral. Do not be intimidated. If you do not care for the doctor's manner, personality, office personnel or anything else, *change doctors!*

Make sure your puppy has a collar, and find out when he'll need a license. (American Eskimo)

Call your local Canine Control Officer or town official to find out at what age your puppy will require a license and what other local laws apply to dogs in your town. Many towns now have leash laws, for example. Ignorance of local ordinances can result in stiff fines. A license (and tag) is usually required for dogs six months of age or over. That tag, along with an ID, should be worn on the dog's regular collar (not the training collar) as a means of identification. Tattooing the dog

provides a permanent, easily read identification that is recorded by the tattoo registry you select to help locate your dog should he ever be lost or stolen. The tattoo is usually done on the inside thigh when the dog is six months of age or older so the numbers will be legible when the dog reaches maturity. The area must then be kept free of hair. The new microchip implant form of identification has its supporters, but to read the "chip" you need a special device, and they're not that readily available.

If you haven't already taken care of them, these are some of the things to put at the top of your "must do" list for tomorrow.

Your New
Puppy's
Needs

What your new puppy needs most is *you*—a responsible person to be at home while Rufus Goofus is learning what he can and can't do. If no one is home to take on this job, the pup has no choice but to teach himself. Puppies are extremely quick to learn, and that is exactly how all puppy problems begin. Left to make his

(Bull Terrier)

own decisions, his idea of what he *can* do is not governed by whether you consider it good or bad.

A puppy looks at things differently: If he is *able* to do it, it must be okay. So he *will* do activities like pulling down the curtains, chewing the rug, spreading the trash or garbage all over the floor, and so on as soon as he discovers he is indeed *able* to and no one is around to prevent his mistakes. Puppies should not be punished for these "normal" (though unacceptable) behaviors, because it is the owner who is at fault for not preventing them.

So let's hope you chose a good time to bring the new puppy home—when whoever is in charge of teaching the pup its first lessons in acceptable family manners is home most of the day. The beginning of a vacation period is a good choice for those who work. But don't panic—read on! There are lots of other things your pup needs.

Food and Water Bowls

**PUPPY
ESSENTIALS**

Your new
puppy will
need:

food bowl

water bowl

collar

leash

I.D. tag

bed

crate

toys

grooming
supplies

Apart from a responsible human being, the puppy needs a variety of basic items. Topping the list are a food dish and a separate water bowl. A mat to put them on is not just for decoration—it will save the floor from slurped water and spilled food. If your pup has long, hanging ears, get dishes specially made to keep such ears out of the food or water. (Saves on cleaning ears twenty times a day and mopping the kitchen when he shakes.) Consider bowls with weighted bases or non-slip bottoms so Rufus can't push them all around the room. For a dog that will be very tall, two dishes in a raised stand will keep food and water where they belong and at a comfortable height.

Lightweight plastic bowls are not a good idea for a teething, chewing puppy. Besides, they are too easily upset. If your puppy is in an exercise pen, a water bowl is available that hangs on the wire and can be raised as the pup grows.

Food

Begin with whatever dog food the breeder was feeding, or ask your veterinarian, or buy a top-quality food made especially for puppies. Veterinarians today agree it is not necessary to add vitamins or minerals to a quality dog food for a healthy puppy. Too many vitamins (especially for large breeds) are actually detrimental.

Don't forget the cookies! Small, plain dog biscuits are fine for "good puppy" rewards and an occasional treat. Fancy flavored treats are okay for adult dogs, but young puppies do better on a blander diet—and fewer treats! (Detailed information on feeding appears in Chapter 4.)

Collar and Leash

There is nothing utilitarian about dog collars and leashes today. They are definitely high fashion, and you'll find them in every imaginable color, with patterns of flowers, stripes or prints, with or without rhinestones or studs, in a variety of fabrics as well as the old standby, braided leather. Before you go overboard, remember that your puppy may go through as many as six different collar sizes as he grows, and a designer item you choose today will probably change over those first eighteen months with the pup's personality or size, or just your latest whim.

A water bowl— with fresh clean water—is essential for your puppy. (Rottweiler)

It is very sad to see a little puppy weighed down with a heavy chain collar and a leash strong enough to restrain a cow! Be sure each collar and leash you select matches the current size and strength of your puppy. (What else they match is up to your mood of the moment.) Take Rufus with you to the pet store to be sure you get the right collar, and just keep in mind that you'll probably be back in a couple of months for a bigger one! The leash will last longer. Unless, of course, Rufus is allowed to use it as a teething toy—definitely *not* a recommended game.

You can put an ID tag on his collar, but he probably won't need a license tag until six months of age (check with your local officials), at which time you will also add a rabies tag. That's a lot of hardware for a small-sized puppy! *Warning:* A training (or "choke") collar should *never* be left on a dog, and especially not on a puppy. Collars that can tighten around the dog's neck are meant to be used only as training devices and removed when the lesson is over. They are not intended for continuous wear because they are dangerous. If this type of collar catches on any immovable object, the dog can

Collars come in all colors and styles, so be creative! Just remember, your puppy will outgrow several collars until she's her full size. (Spinoni Italiano)

easily strangle in its efforts to get free. Stay with soft buckle- or snap-closure collars for everyday wear. If you opt for "motivational training," you'll be staying with the soft collar.

Crate and/or Bed

Your puppy needs a crate. It is a puppy's "bed of choice," a private, personal, snug den where Rufus can sleep, chew a toy and watch the world around him, completely undisturbed. (This is such an important aspect of your puppy's life that much of Chapter 5 is information on the use of a crate.)

Crates come in two styles: closed (fiberglass) or open (wire)—each type has a *plus* and a *minus*. The closed crate is draft-proof, but some pups (and their owners) want to be able to see more. The open variety offers this visibility, but most dogs like the crate covered at bedtime. Either type must be placed away from drafts and sources of heat or air conditioning.

Regardless of which style you decide on, it's important to get the correct size. This is not a puppy playroom or a canine condo. It is basically a bed and the pup will curl up in about one-third of the space. Gauge the adult size of your pup and get a crate that will just allow him to stand and lie down. If that size gives him more space than he needs for the next couple of months, use an adjustable barrier that can be moved back as needed. For large breeds, it may be wiser to have a crate suitable up to six months of age, and then get the one that will last the dog a life-time. (Some breeders will lend a puppy crate, or buy the one you no longer need. Check it out.)

The best puppy bedding is a folded bath towel. It's washable or disposable—accidents happen in the best of homes. If you want a fancy, cuddly bed for your adorable Rufus or Mimi, fine, but count on it just for occasional (supervised) naps in the family room, not while housetraining or for overnight bedtime. Puppies teethe and so they chew. Dog beds are no exception.

A crate is a safe, cozy den for your puppy. (Shetland Sheepdog)

Keeping Puppy Confined

You will need something called an "ex-pen" (read: *playpen*) if your puppy cannot be confined to the kitchen or other safe area by means of doors or gates. The exercise-pen will keep your puppy safe and in one place, but it also allows him room to play, have access to water and use newspapers if he's a latchkey pet with no one home during the day to take him outside.

13

The "gate" mentioned is the good old baby gate, now sold in pet stores as a "pet gate." Choose one that fits your doorway securely, is high enough that the pup can't easily jump over it, and is constructed so the pup won't be encouraged to try his climbing techniques. Some are irresistably chewable, but not if first sprayed with a deterrent such as Grannick's Bitter Apple. The puppy will only accept this device as a barrier if he is taught to respect it as such.

Puppies love and need a variety of toys. (Alaskan Malamute)

Another handy item is a window barrier that enables you to leave a car window partially open when you must leave Rufus in the car (in his crate or seat belt) for a few minutes, or while driving. This also resembles a baby gate, and adjusts to the size of your car window. Speaking of which, the canine seat belt is the latest car safety feature to keep dogs out of the driver's lap or stop them from messing up the game the kids are playing. A worthwhile investment. (*Never leave any dog in any car in warm weather for any length of time. Heatstroke is rapid and fatal.*) When your puppy is older, you may want a back-seat barrier to keep a large dog safely in the back seat of a car or in the back space of a station wagon.

Picker-Uppers

Dog waste has to be disposed of, and there are several easy ways to do it. Pooper scoopers are easy-to-use clean-up tools, and backyard waste systems (that work with natural enzymes) are a popular means of disposal. More and more towns are enforcing ordinances requiring owners to pick up after their dogs in all public areas. All responsible dog owners today carry disposable plastic mitts, or plastic sandwich bags. Put your hand in the bag, pick up the excrement, fold the plastic down over your hand and carry it home or to the nearest trash bin in one of the fashionable fabric zip bags on the market.

Grooming Tools

Your new puppy needs to be groomed at least once or twice a week. Even the Mexican Hairless needs special attention (sunblock, for one thing!). There are special brushes and combs for every type of coat. Most puppies will shed their puppy coat as the adult one grows in. This shedding causes mats in longhaired dogs— and speckled furniture and people's clothing from shorthaired dogs. Definitely, Rufus Goofus needs a brush! He will also need his nails clipped. There are two types of nail trimmers: one uses a scissors action, the other is grimly referred to as a guillotine clipper. Choose whichever one you find comfortable to handle. Either one does the job. ("How to" comes in Chapter 4.)

Toys

Last, but not least according to Rufus, you will need an assortment of appropriate toys—appropriate for his size, age and personal preferences. Safe, fun and interactive doggy toys abound. If your new puppy is your "only child" you'll be tempted to buy one of each. So when you come home with a shopping bag full, give the puppy one or two, possibly add a third later and save the rest for another day. "Variety is the spice of life" applies to dog toys. Every few days, add a new one and subtract an oldie, always letting the favorite toy remain as puppy's security blanket.

One good interactive toy is the red, hard rubber "beehive" toy that bounces erratically when dropped. (The pup will soon learn to drop it himself.) Some balls are meant to be thrown and retrieved; others like the big Boomer ball can be pushed, hit and nosed by the pup alone. A ball with a bell inside maintains interest in the game. Rope toys are great for *mild, controlled* tug-of-war and also for solitary chewing. Rawhides offer hours of chewing, so are more occupational than play. Plush dinosaurs, hedgehogs and numerous other characters produce sounds that range from squeaks to roars. Have fun!

Watch your puppy when he's playing with chew toys, because not every toy is safe for every dog. Some dogs confuse the concept of "play" with "destroy" and are interested only in terminating whatever you buy. Stick with toys that require your participation, or, for solitary play, the larger-sized hard rubber toys and balls and good-sized rawhide bones.

New Puppy *Owner's* Needs

All of the above-mentioned items are available at your local pet store or through pet supply catalogues. There are also some things you, as the owner of a new puppy, will need: A veterinarian (your dog's second-best friend), books and instructional videos about your chosen breed (or dogs in general). The names of a kindergarten puppy trainer, a professional pet sitter, an accredited boarding kennel and a highly recommended groomer.

If you have a backyard, you need a fence. The style can be geared to your home, but the safety factor definitely must be in keeping with the dog's adult size and temperament. If full fencing is not possible, consider a dog run for those dark and stormy nights and crack-of-dawn days when the dog *has* to go out and you'd rather be in bed. Free-standing dog runs are available that can be dismantled and taken along with you should you move. A run won't take the place of daily walks for healthy physical exercise, but it is a great convenience.

Puppy
Proofing
Your Home

To make your home safe for the new puppy will require the same careful preparations as needed for a toddler—in some cases, more so! For example, a toddler might play with a plastic bottle full of a harmful chemical for several minutes before trying to unscrew the top. Extremely dangerous, but a puppy (without benefit  of hands) will instantly puncture the container with sharp, needle-like teeth, making the danger instantaneous.

A toddler won't be tempted over and over again to empty the garbage can. The puppy smells chicken that's in the trash today, so tomorrow the enticement is cheese, the next day hamburger. The association is different each time. The puppy must learn it is the *container* which is off limits. Teach by prevention! Use a guttural *"accht!"* instead of "no." It will sound more like the warning growl from the pup's mother.

Keeping Things out of Reach

Begin with all the obvious precautions. Put all solvents, chemicals, medications and so on out of reach. That means anything you consider potentially harmful,

from mild to wild. That also means such items must be stored higher than the full-grown dog can jump, or behind cupboard doors that cannot be pried open. Paws and noses are incredibly adept at opening almost anything that's closed! The plastic catches sold to keep toddlers out of kitchen cabinets and other storage places work well for dogs, too.

Now is the time to read product labels. If there's a poison warning on the container, be sure everyone in the household knows it and stash the item on a high shelf in the garage or other safe place.

Keeping an eye on your puppy will help keep her out of harm. (Shetland Sheepdog)

Prescription medicines are not the only ones to be guarded. All over-the-counter medications should be kept behind closed doors. You probably don't consider things you use every day for personal hygiene as dangerous, but mouthwash, toothpaste, soap, deodorants and so on are poison to puppies. Be sure to discard the empty containers where the dog can't get at them.

Granted, you can't hide everything you own, or live in an empty shell, so in order to avoid disaster, there are two things you can do. First is to *be aware* of dangers and of what your pup is doing. And the second is to *confine* your puppy whenever you can't keep an eye on him. In other words, use the crate; use pet gates. Putting dangerous items out of reach is merely a simple way to make your job of teaching easier. If all these things are lying around, you'll be saying, "No!" a thousand times a day—and what little puppy wants to hear that? By puppy-proofing your house, you've removed the *dangers* and can proceed with positive training. Muffin will get smiles and praise and learn quickly what she needs to do to earn them. The occasional, necessary "No!" will then have powerful meaning.

Indoors and Outdoors

Protect your puppy from every outside door that does not lead to a safely fenced-in yard. All it takes is for the door to be opened a crack, and the pup can slip through to become another lost dog statistic. Outside, check gates—constantly!

As a protection for muscles, joints and bones, keep the puppy on flooring where he has traction. Slippery floors can cause all kinds of damage to growing pups.

Poisonous Plants

Attractive, innocent-looking plants that you've probably nursed along for years may be poisonous to dogs, particularly puppies—who are in the business of utilizing *all* their senses, including taste.

Some of the common houseplants that are poisonous include ivy, Dieffenbachia (or dumbcane), poinsettia, Jerusalem cherry and philodendron. Once you get outdoors, the list goes on and on, from all bulbs (not necessarily the plant, just the bulb and root system) like daffodils and tulips, to many flowering shrubs and trees.

Among the common garden plants that are especially harmful to puppies (and can be fatal) are foxglove, chrysanthemum leaves, larkspur, ivy, yew, ilex, holly, hydrangea, azalea and many of the wild berry-bearing plants such as elderberry and chokecherry. Mushrooms of every kind, including toadstools, can be fatal.

This warning is not meant to terrify you, but only to inform you so you'll take another look at your garden (indoors and out). As an added precaution against any plants you are not sure about, or ones that you value and don't want chewed or dug up, a European repellent called Get Off My Garden! is now available here. Several similar products are on the market. Check to be sure they are safe for puppies.

Emergency Situations

If your dog vomits up any part of a plant, *it is extremely important to save it for identification in order to ascertain the appropriate treatment to follow.* (Use a plastic poop-pick-up bag or put any plastic bag over your hand, pick up the material and turn the bag down over it.) Some of

the most dangerous poisons are found in the garage: gardening aids such as pesticides or fertilizers, and the number-one killer of pets—anti-freeze, a mere teaspoon of which licked off the garage floor can be fatal.

Know which plants are poisonous and which aren't; accidents do happen, so if he eats something he shouldn't, keep the vet's and poison center's numbers handy. (Golden Retriever)

Being armed with the evidence is one thing, but if you even suspect the pup has ingested a foreign substance, what you do next could save his life. The best thing to do is contact the **National Animal Poison Control Center (NAPCC).** They have a staff of over forty licensed veterinarians and board-certified toxicologists and are available twenty-four hours a day.

There are two ways to reach the NAPCC: If you call 1-800-548-2423, you will be charged $30 per case (on a credit card); there is no charge for follow-up calls. Or you may call 1-900-680-0000 and the charge is $20 for five minutes plus $2.95 for each addition minute (no follow-up). Put both numbers in large, legible print with other emergency telephone numbers. Be prepared to give your name, address and phone number; what your puppy has gotten into (the amount and how long ago); your puppy's breed, age, sex and weight; and what reaction the pup is experiencing.

Considering that NAPCC has been doing this in connection with the University of Illinois since 1978, and receives over 30,000 calls a year, the danger of poisoning is very real.

Protecting the Plants

Here's an easy way to keep your pup away from large potted house plants. Put aluminum foil around the pot, extending up to cover the lower foliage. Then take the added precaution of spraying the foil and any exposed leaves with Grannick's Bitter Apple Plant and Leaf Protector.

Watch closely what your puppy is doing while you are weeding the veggies. *Teach* puppy the boundaries of your gardens by walking him around on leash (so you have instant control to prevent a misstep). This lesson, by the way, in no way guarantees that your puppy now or two years from now will walk sedately down the path while the squirrel he's pursuing dashes through the flower bed! Even the Father of our Country took down a cherry tree in a weak moment.

It's up to you to make sure your puppy can't get into things he shouldn't, like the trash can. (Shetland Sheepdog)

Other Small Creatures

Your kids have a couple of hamsters, so what precautions are in order? Several, but they all boil down to one thing: *separation*. No matter how sweet, dear and adorable little Fifi the Poodle may be, she is first and foremost a dog. And dogs do not tolerate little creatures like mice, gerbils and hamsters. Chase is the name of the game, and "catch" is the sad end of it.

Be very sure the kids understand that their other pets must never (*never*) be out of their cages if the puppy is in the room or can push its way into the room. Despite magazine pictures you see to the contrary, the species do not instinctively mix socially. (Those photos are carefully posed with highly trained animals by exceptional trainers!)

Cats

Cats and kittens can be carefully introduced to dogs (preferably older cats to puppies, kittens to adult dogs) and even after a rocky start, most will settle down. They will either become bosom buddies, or a love-hate relationship will keep them forever at a safe distance. Their owners learn to live with it.

Introduce the two by leaving the pup in his crate to allow the cat time to investigate. When that much goes off without too much hissing or barking, hold the puppy in your lap and let the cat proceed with feline caution. Do *not* hold the kitty or you could be scratched to pieces! Be careful, too, that the pup doesn't get scratched around the eyes or face. (Wash the area immediately and thoroughly if this happens.)

Generally the cat will run off (or more accurately, run *up*) to where it feels safe, leaving the puppy deprived of the chase. If so, good. Puppy has learned that cats play by different rules.

Knick-Knacks

Puppies have no idea of material values, and it's strange how few people realize this until it's too late. Put your precious china ornaments up high (or away) if a long tail will wipe them off the coffee table. Remove the Persian rug from the hallway where you won't see it being chewed or urinated on. Lift up (or disconnect) lampcords and

---

HOUSEHOLD DANGERS

Curious puppies and inquisitive dogs get into trouble not because they are bad, but simply because they want to investigate the world around them. It's our job to protect our dogs from harmful substances, like the following:

IN THE HOUSE

cleaners, especially pine oil

perfumes, colognes, aftershaves

medications, vitamins

office and craft supplies

electric cords

chicken or turkey bones

chocolate

some house and garden plants, like ivy, oleander and poinsettia

IN THE GARAGE

antifreeze

garden supplies, like snail and slug bait, pesticides, fertilizers, mouse and rat poisons

TV and radio wires that could be chewed or appliances pulled down when you're on the phone or in the shower. Fold back ends of runners or tablecloths that hang over the edge ready to be yanked in the blink of an eye.

Treat your new puppy like a toddler and be thankful that he will learn acceptable behavior in a matter of months, or almost as quickly as you can teach him. A puppy goes from toddler to teen to adult in about two years.

Your
Growing

part two

Puppy

chapter 4

Food, Exercise
and Overall
Care

(Golden Retriever)

There is not much your puppy wants more than his food. Apart from you, that is! Since you are The Source of food, you score twice. You need to know how a puppy views food, because fussy or problem eaters are generally *made,* not *born.* Rapidly growing puppies have an intense desire as well as the obvious need to be fed—a puppy has to eat in order to grow. But the "desire" is a sure-fire way for the puppy to go after attention, and that's where your teaching comes in. If you fall for all the puppy's cute, darling and adorable ways to beg for food, you will have a nuisance-begger for years to come.

So, correctly used, food is a ready-made teaching tool. You can use it to teach a lot more than table manners. Feeding your puppy goes well beyond putting a bowl of dog food on the floor. Always ask for something in return—a sit, a paw, a say "please" or whatever—but let the puppy know food comes with a price.

Where to Feed

Pick a place to feed your puppy that is in a non-traffic area of the kitchen, then stick to that one spot. The water bowl stays there. The food dish is put down and removed after fifteen to twenty minutes. Dogs like to know exactly where and when meals will be served day after day. Now we've established *where* to feed; next is *when*, *what* and *how much*.

When to Feed

For the first few days, stay with whatever feeding schedule your puppy has been on so you don't upset his internal clock. Some kennels and breeders use what is called the "self-feeding" method, which means a large amount of food is put out and the pup eats at will all day long. This method is *not* recommended for several reasons, the first of which is that puppies tend to overeat. Pups of large breeds allowed to eat at will tend to grow too quickly and run the risk of bone disease. Smaller breeds risk becoming obese.

Apart from those health-related reasons, a puppy left alone all day with access to food tends to overeat out of sheer boredom. And a puppy

TYPES OF FOODS/TREATS

There are three types of commercially available dog food—dry, canned and semimoist—and a huge assortment of treats (lucky dogs!) to feed your dog. Which should you choose?

Dry and canned foods contain similar ingredients. The primary difference between them is their moisture content. The moisture is not just water. It's blood and broth, too, the very things that dogs adore. So while canned food is more palatable, dry food is more economical, convenient and effective in controlling tartar buildup. Most owners feed a 25% canned/75% dry diet to give their dogs the benefit of both. Just be sure your dog is getting the nutrition he needs (you and your veterinarian can determine this).

Semimoist foods have the flavor dogs love and the convenience owners want. However, they tend to contain excessive amounts of artificial colors and preservatives.

Dog treats come in every size, shape and flavor imaginable, from organic cookies shaped like postmen to beefy chew sticks. Dogs seem to love them all, so enjoy the variety. Just be sure not to overindulge your dog. Factor treats into her regular meal sizes.

that's allowed to eat all day long also needs to eliminate "all day long," making housetraining difficult, to say the least.

On top of all that, you lose your role as provider, the offer of food ceases to be an exciting event, and food rewards lose their effectiveness as teaching tools. So, if your pup came home on a self-feed schedule, take the next two or three days to put him on the more normal three-times-a-day routine.

As far as how many meals to give, from eight to twelve weeks, feed the puppy four times a day. Avoid feeding late at night by working on a schedule of 7 A.M., 11 A.M. (or noon), 3 P.M. and 6 P.M. At about twelve weeks, eliminate the afternoon meal and—for small to medium breeds—reduce it to two meals a day at six months. Large breeds can remain on three meals a day until twelve or even eighteen months due to the danger of bloat from eating too much food at one time.

What to Feed

You are feeding a rapidly growing puppy not to satisfy his appetite, but to have him become as healthy an adult dog as possible. The extra you pay for a premium puppy food could end up saving you large sums of money later in health care costs.

Small-to-medium breeds are fed a growth (or puppy) food three times

HOW TO READ THE DOG FOOD LABEL

With so many choices on the market, how can you be sure you are feeding the right food for your dog? The information is all there on the label—if you know what you're looking for.

Look for the nutritional claim right up top. Is the food "100% nutritionally complete"? If so, it's for nearly all life stages; "growth and maintenance," on the other hand, is for early development; puppy foods are marked as such, as are foods for senior dogs.

Ingredients are listed in descending order by weight. The first three or four ingredients will tell you the bulk of what the food contains. Look for the highest-quality ingredients, like meats and grains, to be among them.

The Guaranteed Analysis tells you what levels of protein, fat, fiber and moisture are in the food, in that order. While these numbers are meaningful, they won't tell you much about the quality of the food. Nutritional value is in the dry matter, not the moisture content.

In many ways, seeing is believing. If your dog has bright eyes, a shiny coat, a good appetite and a good energy level, chances are his diet's fine. Your dog's breeder and your veterinarian are good sources of advice if you're still confused.

a day until they are about six months of age, when you can cut back to feeding twice a day. Usually, a puppy will begin to leave some or most of the midday meal as an indication that it is no longer needed. When a pup has reached ninety percent of his full height (between nine to twelve months of age), it's time to switch to a maintenance diet that provides fewer calories.

Large breeds such as German Shepherd Dogs, Golden or Labrador Retrievers can be switched over to a maintenance diet sooner in order to slow down their rate of growth since they take longer to mature (twelve to twenty-four months).

Offer your puppy her food at regular times during the day; don't just leave a bowl out for the whole day. (Great Dane)

Which Food Is Best

Keep your puppy on the same food he has been eating *unless* it is not a top commercial brand dog food especially formulated for puppies; or if your vet advises a different food; or if your puppy is not doing well (check with the vet first). Then, and only then, a change is in order.

Your puppy's veterinarian will recommend a quality puppy food if you are confused by the array on the store shelves. Make the switch gradually over a period of three or four days to avoid stress or stomach upsets, and do it by *substituting*—not adding! Replace a small amount of the original food with the new. Increase the amount of new food each day, as you decrease the unwanted one, until the change is complete.

Most breeders and canine nutritionists today agree that what's best for the dog—and what the dog likes best—is a combination of one-quarter canned meat mixed with three-quarters kibble (or dry) dog food. The meat is good for them and adds the taste and scent dogs enjoy, which in turn encourages sluggish eaters. The majority of healthy puppies, however,

tend to "inhale" their food, and the kibble slows them down, gives them chewing exercise and also helps to reduce tartar accumulation on the molars (or crushing teeth). But for an eight- to twelve-week-old puppy of a small breed, you could soak the kibble in a little warm water to soften it for tiny teeth, changing to dry as permanent teeth erupt.

Puppy or "growth" commercial formulas contain all the vitamins and minerals required by growing pups of all breeds or sizes. Adding more will upset the balance and cause dietary problems. For example, the correct proportion of calcium and phosphorus necessary for good bone growth is in a

Specially formulated puppy foods contain all the nutrients a growing dog needs. (Bull Terrier)

quality growth food. Don't be tempted to add any vitamins or mineral supplements. Instead of helping, you could be doing irreparable harm.

Digestibility is important and something you can easily check. If as much is coming out of the dog as is going in, he is not assimilating enough nourishment. Unfortunately, reading labels will only tell you the quantity, and not the quality. For example, the source of *chicken* could be from the breast or feet; of *beef* from rib steak or the intestines.

All canned dog food, due to its high moisture content, can go bad quickly, so refrigerate leftovers. For a young puppy, warm it up slightly—at least to room temperature—before serving. The canned *meat with gravy* means you are paying for a large portion (about eighty percent) of moisture containing little or no nutritional value. The canned chopped meat, or meat and rice, formulated for puppies is a better choice. The shelves are loaded with choices, but in the beginning, stay with one brand, one variety. That way you will know if the pup is vomiting because his stomach can't handle a certain food or due to something more serious. Save a gourmet menu for the adult dog.

There is another category of foods called semi-moist, made to look like the real thing—hamburger, ground chicken or steak. They are handy for camping trips with an adult dog, but are not recommended for puppies since they are high in caloric content and can cause tartar build-up.

How Much to Feed

The feeding instructions on bags and cans of commercial dog foods are often too generous. Be guided by the fact that a young puppy will consume what its stomach can comfortably hold in about fifteen to twenty minutes, after which remove the dish. Do not leave it longer than that. This is The Source (you) at work, establishing good eating habits!

You'll know you're feeding him right if your puppy's coat is glossy, his eyes are bright, and he looks good all over. (Samoyed)

A good guide, however, is your puppy's appearance. His coat should be glossy, his eyes bright and clear, his teeth coming in straight and free of tartar. You should be able to feel his ribs. A puppy that is too round and roly-poly is unhealthy. The puppy could have internal parasites or just too many calories. Fresh clean water is every bit as important as food and should be available at all times.

But puppies, like people, are individuals, eating habits included—just be sure you're not being conned!

Most puppies are convinced they are starving. Those pathetic whines and soulful eyes pleading for seconds (or dessert) could be masking a full stomach! Obesity is the Number One nutritional disorder in dogs of all ages. A puppy does not need diet food, but he does need diet management. Be sure the kids understand that puppies do not get pieces of jelly doughnuts, hamburger rolls, fries or other goodies under the table. Speaking of kids and goodies, remind everyone that chocolate is poisonous to dogs.

What If the Puppy Doesn't Like the Food?

Perhaps *you* are seeing a problem that doesn't exist. A puppy that doesn't eat *any food at all* for twenty-four hours should be taken to the veterinarian. No healthy

puppy that is offered food three or four times a day (and has it removed after fifteen minutes) ever starved. Dogs are manipulative, but not stupid! Conversely, a dog that eats well but appears to be genuinely hungry all day in between meals should be checked by your veterinarian.

Treats Treats equate with love: they are just as pleasurable to give as to receive. Just be sure you (and everyone else in the house-

When she's old enough, you may want to replace a meal with a dog biscuit; always consider treats part of your pup's complete diet.
(Nova Scotia Duck Tolling Retriever)

hold) realize that treats are food. They should be doled out in tiny portions. If you reward your puppy with a treat and he lies down to chew it, it was probably too large. Consider it part of his dinner. A true treat is a reward that's small enough to be swallowed after one crunch. It's a taste.

The "goodnight, good dog" biscuit (more about that later) is a case in point. It is part of the pup's daily quota of food. When puppy grows up, you may decide to replace breakfast with a dog biscuit, an excellent solution for the overweight or under-exercised dog.

Bones Just say No to bones. If you insist your dog needs a bone, buy a large sterilized bone at the pet store. Bones were given to dogs in the past because they satisfied the dog's need to chew and gnaw, and a bone from the butcher (or the dinner table) was all there was to give them. This was also before people worried about the dangers of splintered bones stuck in the throat or intestinal tract, costing hundreds of dollars to remove. And long before anyone even thought about making toys especially for pets!

Dog Food Do's and Don'ts

Do keep small children away from the puppy while he's eating. A puppy is in the process of being taught that he does not have to guard food. Little kids are thought by the dog to be a real threat because they are so close to the dish! Puppies often consider young children as littermates and therefore competitors, especially for food. Play it safe. A puppy (or adult dog) may accept the child squatting down to watch him eat today, only to retaliate tomorrow.

Children are bitten because they do not understand the importance of food to an animal, and because the kids and the pups have not been taught that a danger exists. An older child of seven or eight will want to feed the puppy herself, but she still needs to be taught exactly how to do it, and that includes keeping a hands-off safe distance once the dog is eating.

From the beginning, show your pup that you are The Source of food and you are not to be messed with! Get him to watch you take out a few kibbles before you put his dish on the floor. Then let him eat them, as a treat, out of your hand—gently. If he nips or snatches, close your hand and stand up. Use the word "gentle" *as* he's licking your fingers. Then tell him "good dog."

When he has learned to sit on command, he can do that before you put the dish down. Keeping your hand beside the dish for a moment establishes trust. If there's one growl or snarl, the dish is removed and Rufus is put back on a sit. Release him, wait a few

33

minutes and repeat the whole process. He's a smart puppy. He'll quickly catch onto your lesson in table manners!

In everything you do with and for your puppy, remember that you are teaching him. You are teaching him what you want him to do, how to do it and that he can trust the people in his new family. Food is a major lesson in trust. A dog can't fix his own meals, so he must *trust* you to do it, which is why consistency is so important. Same times, same place, same food.

Fresh, clean water must be available until bedtime. That is just as important as food.

Your puppy learned to play with his littermates; now you have to take over. (Golden Retriever)

Exercise

Beyond food in importance to your puppy's growth (and pleasure) is exercise. Puppy workouts take many forms, some solo, some with members of his new family. Play, eat and sleep are what puppies do best. (Okay. Add piddle and poop.) A puppy can play alone, but the games they shared with their littermates were more fun, and now the new members of the family take on the role of playmates.

Jogging and running are *not* the right kind of exercise for a puppy, not even a big puppy. In fact, the larger the dog will be, the more you need to limit his physical exercise (including jogging, running and jumping) until maturity. Have your veterinarian check the dog for soundness (heart, hips, etc.) at twelve to eighteen months. Dogs will always *try* to keep up with you, to perform whatever you ask them to do, so it is up to you to set the limits. Leaping over hurdles, two-mile trots and flying Frisbee catches are for full-grown, physically sound adults, not puppies.

Puppies get most of their exercise from energetic play with four feet on the ground. Chase is a favorite because it is instinctive, so whether the "prey" is a large and indestructible Boomer ball for a Rottie puppy or a small squeaky rolled on the floor for a Yorkie, the game is the same.

Roughhousing

While still with his litter-mates, your puppy learned to roughhouse. It's a great game, but don't get carried away! All physical interaction between you and your puppy should be at the pup's level of strength, ability and understanding. A young puppy is just learning to trust, and if unintentionally hurt, will probably come back at you with teeth, which is just what he would do to a littermate. Don't punish. Apologize however you like, offer a quick tummy-rub to show there's no hard feelings, and get on with less strenuous play. Over-stimulation is stressful and can lead to aggressive behavior. Know when to quit—*before* play becomes frantic, *before* the pup is exhausted, *before* there's more biting than mouthing.

Exercise is as important as food, and often as pleasurable for the pup. (Samoyed)

If the puppy's activities have gone too far, steady him by holding him gently (but firmly) in a sit as you say very calmly and firmly, "Settle" (or "steady" or "chill out" or whatever you like so long as it is the *same* every

35

time). For a large, out-of-control puppy, lead him quietly to his crate for a Time-Out. Let him out after two or three minutes and only while he is quiet. After all that, he will probably need to pee.

Just because you've got a short-haired breed, don't think you can skip grooming! (Beagle)

Walking the Dog

There are different kinds of walks. One is the "bathroom break" or "business trip," which really isn't a walk at all. The puppy is on lead and is taken to the place where he's meant to relieve himself.

Another kind of walk is the training variety. Puppy is on lead and be-bopping all over the place while you try to get him to follow you. Eventually he does and with lots of practice, you'll both graduate to the next two kinds of walks.

The "exercise walk" is the one we see so often these days. The person is getting his or her muscle tone up and excess fat down, and it is a very intense, no-nonsense, nonstop regimen. Dogs go along because they don't have a choice. This walk is strictly for adults. Puppies need not apply. All exercise should be curtailed in warm weather and even eliminated when it gets hot. Heat stroke is dangerous at best, fatal at worst. Prevention is the best cure.

But then there is the "dog's walk," the one where Rufus gets to sniff everything along the way, to stop to greet other dogs and people, perhaps stop to buy a newspaper or feed the ducks. It is pure pleasure, the stuff canine heaven must be made of, and what's more, it is also very good for Rufus's owner. It is a calming form of exercise and allows you to teach-as-you-go. Rufus learns to greet other dogs nicely, not jump up when you greet friends, to sit or stand quietly when patted and admired.

For now this walk comes under the heading of "socializing your puppy," but this is the truly companionable walk that begins in puppyhood and is never outgrown.

Grooming

Maybe you think you can skip this section because you have a smooth-coated puppy that you've been told doesn't need to be groomed. Wrong! *All* dogs must be groomed. As a bonus, your puppy will learn that it's okay to have someone go over every inch of his body, and there will be no trauma or stress when being examined by the vet, worked on by a professional groomer or a trainer, or perhaps eventually given the once-over by an obedience trial judge. Besides, dogs think they are *Very Special* when they've had grooming attention.

WHERE TO GROOM

Begin with the puppy off the ground. About waist-high is a comfortable height to work. If you try to groom a dog on the ground, he has the advantage—you're on *his* turf and he's faster on four feet than you are! Get him up off the floor and *you* will be in control. If you don't have a grooming table, use any sturdy table, workbench or countertop. Add a mat (a car floormat or thin rubber doormat are both good choices) so the pup will feel secure and won't slip.

To get your pup used to brushes, you can let them lie in your lap, but you'll eventually want to groom your dog standing up.
(Shetland Sheepdog)

In a pet supply store you can get a grooming arm that clamps onto any tabletop and which, with a noose, will help keep the dog in place. There is always the danger of a puppy (or an adult dog) stepping off the edge of the grooming area, so get in the habit of keeping one hand (and both eyes) on the pup at all times, especially if you use a grooming noose.

A very tiny puppy—especially one with a long coat—may be brushed the first time or two lying in your lap so the pup is comfortable while you practice using the brush and comb. Grooming dogs (even puppies) with long coats does take time, so these puppies have to be taught to lie quietly on either side while you work. It's a struggle at first, but soon the dog will use the time to catch a nap.

Keep these first grooming sessions short. *Very* short—ten minutes, max. Always stop when the puppy is behaving nicely. *Never* end a session because the puppy is whining, growling, barking, biting or acting up. If you do, you will have taught him that he can dictate when the time is up. Instead, just go right on grooming, but do something he really likes in order to settle him down, add a "good dog" when the behavior is again acceptable, and *then* quit.

GROOMING TOOLS

You also need the right tools for the job. For a smooth-coated pup, you need a soft bristle brush, a sisal mitt or a rubber curry brush to stimulate the skin to keep it healthy and to distribute the natural oils in the coat. A good comb for a short-haired puppy is a double-toothed flea comb (one side has finer teeth than the other). It will pull out any foreign objects like ticks, fleas or burrs.

For a puppy with a thick, long or wire coat, you will need a metal comb and a brush made for your puppy's type of coat. If you missed that information when you got your puppy, a groomer or the pet store will help you choose the right ones. Pet supply catalogs also list pages of these grooming tools, many of which are designed specifically for certain breeds. If you decide on a "slicker" (or bent-wire) brush, get the "soft" type for a puppy. Use it gently and only through the hair because the wire will scratch the skin if you get carried away.

There are several types of tools made to break up mats, as well as special shedding tools for both long- and short-haired dogs. Something for everyone!

Trimming Nails

Nails need to be trimmed regularly, and there are two basic types of trimmers to consider. One works like a regular scissors, and the other slices the nail guillotine-fashion when the two spring-operated handles are squeezed. Nail trimmers are made for small dogs (or puppies) and for big dogs whose large nails require a strong implement to do the job.

Only the tip that grows out beyond the quick is cut. On white nails, the quick is easier to see than on black nails. If you cut into the quick, it will bleed profusely. Styptic powder stops the bleeding, but it stings and the puppy won't be thrilled to let you cut nails the next time! Some dogs have an extra nail called a dewclaw on the inside of the leg above the foot. Dewclaws must be trimmed, too.

Your vet or groomer can show you how to cut nails, or, if you are really not keen to learn how, then regular trips to the groomer's for nail trimming are in order. Overgrown nails can cause a variety of problems from painful walking to deformities requiring surgery. Puppies are wiggly, but their nails are thinner and easier to cut than those of an adult dog. Start now with a weekly schedule and by the time your pup is fully grown, you will both have conquered the nail-trimming technique.

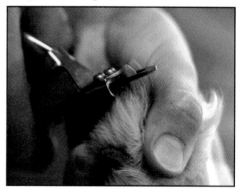

Regular nail trimming is important for the health of your dog's feet; just make sure you don't clip into the quick!

Brushing

Brushing is done from the skin out to the ends of the hairs, slowly and methodically on long-haired dogs. A mistake most people make is only to brush the ends or

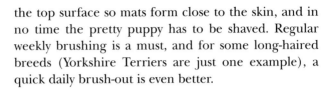
the top surface so mats form close to the skin, and in no time the pretty puppy has to be shaved. Regular weekly brushing is a must, and for some long-haired breeds (Yorkshire Terriers are just one example), a quick daily brush-out is even better.

Mats begin with a few snarled hairs and are found most often under the front legs (behind the elbow) and behind the ears. Work them out slowly and gently, first pulling the hairs apart with your fingers (or using the end tooth of the metal comb to pick the hairs apart), combing and brushing them straight as you go. A fine mist of plain water will reduce static electricity, which can hamper the job. Mats do not go away. They just get rapidly worse! If they are getting even slightly ahead of you, phone the groomer.

Regular brushing and cleaning of the ears and eyes will keep your puppy looking—and feeling—its best. (Collie)

Ear Care

Using a clean dampened cloth, wipe the inside flap of the puppy's ears. The inside of the ear has a natural light coating of wax that should not be removed. If the ear is really dirty (a long walk on a dusty road might do it), dampen a piece of gauze or cotton in mineral oil and gently wipe out the dirt. Be careful not to push dirt further into the ear. If there is a foul odor or excessive wax, consult your veterinarian. *Never* go into the ear with a cotton swab—ever!

Eye Care

Clean around the eyes using a cotton ball dampened in clean warm water—one for each eye. Gently wipe away any accumulation of debris, but take the opportunity to check for mucus discharge, healthy eyelids and clear, healthy-looking eyes.

Don't back off if your puppy objects to any portion of the grooming or he'll object more strenuously the next time. Anything from excessive wriggling to a snap or growl is corrected with an "Aaacht!" and then continue grooming, but switch to a nearby spot. For example, if this happens when you're cleaning out an ear, correct and then with your fingers gently massage just in back of the ear. Next time, *begin* with the comforting massage before getting on with the cleaning.

Tending to Teeth

The first, or puppy, teeth of course fall out and the permanent set will erupt starting at about four or five months of age, at which time gums may be tender. Before then, get your puppy accustomed to your fingers going into his mouth. Gently lift his lips, one side at a time, and rub gently along the gums with your finger wrapped in a piece of gauze dampened with water. When he accepts that much, add a little canine toothpaste to the gauze. *People toothpaste is harmful to dogs.* There are several canine varieties on the market. You can use a regular soft-bristled toothbrush, but there are also special ones for dogs as well as pads to use on your index finger, or a small brush that fits on your finger. Or you can continue to use surgical gauze.

Teeth need to be brushed twice a week to maintain dental health (which is very expensive to repair!). This routine allows you to keep tabs on how the permanent teeth are erupting and whether or not your veterinarian needs to be alerted to any abnormality.

Anal Sacs

It's a mystery why dogs secrete dark brown anal sac fluid with its horrendous odor. It may be to mark territory, but that's a guess because the good news is that most dogs do not have this problem. There is one anal sac on either side of the anus at approximately five and seven o'clock. You'll know anal sacs are the culprits if the dog is frantically trying to bite his tail or lick the area while dragging his backside on the ground.

Your veterinarian will first want to be sure the sacs are not infected or impacted. If not, he will probably express them for you—it is not a job anyone volunteers for! And if it will need to be done again, you'll be shown how.

Using Shampoo/Bathing

You *may* shampoo a young puppy, but it's better not to unless there is a valid reason, such as a bad case of fleas. However, it is hard to resist giving a little white ball of fluff a beauty treatment. First, thoroughly brush out the dog's coat. Mats will be impossible to untangle later. Put a cotton ball in each ear to keep the water out, and a drop of mineral oil in each eye.

Frequent shampooing can deplete the natural oils in your dog's coat. With regular overall grooming, your pup should look and smell fine. (Great Dane)

Work in a warm room. Use quite warm water (the pup's body temperature is higher than yours) and only use shampoo or flea products made specifically for puppies. Put a towel in the sink or tub for safe footing, and use a spray attachment to help get out every bit of soap. You cannot rinse too much. Towel dry and/or blow dry with a hair dryer set on warm, *not* hot, and held at least eighteen inches or more away from the dog. Brush the coat carefully as it dries to avoid snarls and that enemy of long hair, mats.

Frequent shampooing destroys the natural oils in a dog's coat and can lead to dry skin problems. With good grooming habits, including rinsing off muddy feet, most dogs do not need a bath more than once a year. The exception would be any of the long-coated breeds, especially those that require professional trimming.

The point of grooming a new puppy is to get him used to being handled, to enjoy the hands-on physical attention. The results—beautification and health—are secondary benefits. In the process of grooming, your hands will find a tick or a lump that wasn't there last time, and your eyes will see fleas, a runny nose, tartar on teeth and other indications of your pup's health. It's not just grooming. What you're doing amounts to teaching, bonding and preventive medicine!

chapter **5**

Housetraining

Housetraining is sometimes called house*breaking*. It's easy to see how that word gets confused with all kinds of other things puppies do, none of which are what any owner of a new puppy has in mind! So "housetraining" it is, and it begins the minute you walk in the door with your new puppy. (It is almost impossible to housetrain a puppy that is infested with worms, so a speedy vet-check for worms is a must.)

Using a Crate

When a new puppy comes to your home, it's prime time for using a crate. This essential piece of canine equipment is described in Chapter 2. Housetraining begins with the crate. Call it a crate or a bed or a den, but not a "cage" (that's a four-letter word); it is your

44

pup's home at home or away, his refuge in times of stress (yours or his) and an ideal spot for an undisturbed nap. It is an invaluable tool for housetraining.

The kitchen is the area you are most likely to choose for puppy confinement, so during the day that is where to put the crate. At night, move the crate into your bedroom. (More on confinement later.) Pick a spot in the kitchen that is accessible to the puppy and to you and leave the crate door open so the pup can go in and out. When you want him to stay put, you close it.

As soon as you arrive home with the puppy, take him out *on leash* to the small area where you want him to eliminate. This can be behind a bush in the garden, on crushed stone in a dog run, or beside the curb in the city. It is essential to keep the pup on leash!

Each and every person who is involved in housetraining the puppy needs to understand the "*how*" and the "*why*" of the rules.

Establishing Rules

On leash is the first answer to *how*. You are *not* taking the puppy for a walk. Walks come later. Consider this a "business trip." Take him to his spot (of your choosing) and stand there. No chit-chat. Pretend not even to look at him. Occasionally a pup will decide to sit while you stand (they know more obedience stuff than you think!). If that happens, just take a few steps this way and that to get Rufus moving about. This part takes time, but it's time well spent.

As to *why*, there are several reasons. For starters, the leash prevents the puppy from taking off on a game of "chase-me." The major reason, however, is that the leash keeps you beside the puppy so you can say "good dog" *as* he eliminates. Food rewards are inappropriate. All the puppy needs is your approval.

The timing of everything you say or do to a puppy— whether it is praise, a preventive warning or a correction—must be done *as that specific action occurs.* Praising the pup after he has relieved himself only tells him you *approve of the way he is now walking*. Obviously, that's not what you meant!

Dogs like to have one designated area in which to relieve themselves. (It's up to you to keep it clean, by the way.) Once the pup catches on to eliminating there, you can add a command word if you like. Say "Go-potty" (or whatever one-word term you wish) *as* you reach the spot. You'll get plenty of practice—at eight to ten weeks, pups need to eliminate about every two hours.

By now you're exhausted, but take a few minutes to play outdoors, or back inside. When the puppy is older, this will be a good time for a walk.

SOME DO'S AND DON'TS

Don't return to the room if the crated pup is fussing.

Don't let him out of the crate while he's complaining.

Do let him eliminate first if he will be crated for an hour or more.

Don't blame the puppy for accidents you could have prevented.

Don't use the crate for punishment.

Do withhold water for two or three hours before bedtime.

Do remind children that the dog's crate is off-limits.

Don't feed the puppy in the crate.

Don't let your puppy think his name is "NO!"

Don't nag.

Introducing the Crate

We're going to backtrack here in order to clear up the matter of introducing your puppy to the joys of a crate. Puppies are programmed by Mother Nature to keep their den clean, so all you have to do is to provide the "den" (crate) and stick to a schedule that allows your puppy to maintain that goal of cleanliness. Rufus Goofus may already have learned all about a crate and need nothing more than to know where you keep it. Lucky you! For the rest of the new puppy owners, here's the procedure.

Don't worry if the puppy is more cautious than curious at first. He's being sensible about something that might be dangerous! Do *not* push, shove or in any way try to force him into the crate. The situation calls for the art of gentle persuasion. Sweet-talk him into overcoming his doubts by interesting him in a toy and then tossing it into the crate. Or let him see and sniff a small treat in your hand *as* your hand goes into the crate. (Where a yummy treat goes, a pup is sure to follow.) *As* one paw steps inside, add the now-familiar "good dog—good **crate**!"

Slowly but Surely

Leave the door open for now, and if he does an instant turnaround (or backs out unceremoniously), that's normal. Make no comment, because Rufus is never praised for coming *out*, only for going in. Repeat this little scenario until the pup trots right in by himself. *Every* time you catch him about to step into the crate, be ready to say, "good dog—good **crate**." Even if he's just looking for crumbs, it means he has accepted the idea that the crate is his own place. That's your goal.

After you've taken your puppy outside, take a few minutes to play with her. (Shiba Inu)

Now begin to lure him into the crate with a toy or a treat and close the door. Say "good dog" or "good crate" and then ignore him completely. Now is a good time to peel potatoes, read junk mail or just pretend you're busy.

If Rufus reacts by whining, or howling like a banshee, give the top of the crate a sharp tap *as* you say, "NO! Quiet!" Then go back to the potatoes. (If you keep glancing toward the crate, he *will* fuss. That's a given.) You are catching onto the "*as*" timing, aren't you?

Open the door to let Rufus out only when he is quiet— or even asleep. Gradually increase the length of time

47

he stays in the crate with the door closed until you reach half an hour or more. As the time increases, begin going in and out of the room, varying the amount of time you are in or out.

The exception to this crate-training process is overnight. From the first night, take the puppy out last thing before your bedtime, then put him in the crate in your bedroom (tempt him with a small biscuit) and close the crate door. *No* conversation. He'll settle down if you ignore him. It's been a very busy day.

First thing in the morning—at the very first sound from Rufus— pick up the leash and Rufus (or lead him, if he's too big to carry) to his spot and wait. It shouldn't take long this time. Then into his confined area. Or, maybe on a weekend morning, back into his crate with a small biscuit.

Indoor Rules

Once you are back indoors, don't make the common mistake of letting the puppy run free all over your house. That kind of freedom means only one thing: "freedom to get into trouble" and "freedom to be punished" because puppies on their own *will* get into trouble. Confinement to one room or one area in a room is actually being kind to your puppy.

Your puppy may associate having to relieve himself with the door and may start to ask to go out on his own. (Shetland Sheepdog)

If you can't keep an eye on him, let him relieve himself, offer fresh water and then the puppy can go into his crate, go "free" in his confined area with a couple of toys, or go to sleep. Puppies need a lot of sleep because they are growing so fast.

When he wakes up, he'll need to go outside to eliminate. Take advantage of his need and teach him there's a word for it. "You have to go *outside? Outside?*" Bear in mind that after the puppy urinates, he will have to defecate, so don't make the mistake of returning to the house too soon. It is even normal for a puppy to move his bowels twice within a few minutes. Be sure he has finished and you'll have prevented an accident.

Stick to the Schedule

Then it's the same routine: on-leash outside, followed by playtime, followed by food, water, another nap, and then—surprise—outside again! That's how the puppy's day goes. You will soon learn how often he needs to relieve himself and to watch for the telltale circling, whining or pawing that precedes it. (If you're too late, or almost too late, get him out the door and snap the leash on when you get there!)

As the amount you feed decreases, and the meals are cut from three to two and possibly to one, and as the ability of your puppy to control his bodily functions increases, the fewer trips outside he'll need.

> **TIPS FOR CITY DOGS**
>
> Carry a small puppy in the elevator or up and down stairs. A puppy too big to carry is still a puppy, so protect him in the elevator by letting him sit in the corner with you standing in front of him so he won't get stepped on.
>
> Keep your coat and the leash handy. First thing in the morning can be very early!
>
> City street noises can be frightening to a puppy. Find as secluded a spot as possible in which to curb your pup. Take plastic baggies with you and do your part to keep your city clean.

When the puppy lets you know he has to go out, and when the meals are cut back to two, begin to let him outside on his own but watch from a window if possible. Promote him too soon and your clever puppy will diddle you by playing around outdoors, barking to be let in—and will promptly have an accident on your best carpet. Your fault, not his.

Don't scold a puppy for having had an accident. It's past tense—remember the "*as*" rule. It's up to you to *prevent* accidents and also to accept the fact that you are only human and you can't prevent everything!

Paper Training

If everyone leaves the house in the morning and returns six to eight hours later, you have several options. You can ask a friend, neighbor or professional pet sitter to take the puppy out for an hour in the middle of the day (and feed him, and take him out again), or you can paper-train.

Leave several thicknesses of newspaper in one corner of the area the puppy is confined to when you are out—in one corner of an ex-pen away from his water dish and his bed, or in one corner by the back door, for example. Warning: If you paper the entire floor (or even too large an area), the puppy will *use* the entire area, probably by turning at least half of it into confetti. Boredom has a way of expressing itself.

When your pup has gone a couple of months without having an accident inside, you can safely say he's housetrained. (American Water Spaniel)

On your return, put (or take) the puppy outside as usual, and clean up the newspapers in silence. That gives the pup the message that what he did is okay, but only okay, nothing to warrant either praise or disapproval.

When the time comes to do without papers, gradually diminish the papered area. Many people who must leave their adult dogs alone all day routinely put newspapers down, just in case. Better a soiled newspaper than a damaged bladder.

When Is He Housetrained?

When your puppy has been accident-free for several days, you're on your way. When the puppy has been clean for a couple of months and routinely asks to be taken out, you are just about there. But keep in mind that your puppy cannot have perfect control at all times under all circumstances. Some puppies will still have an occasional accident between six months and a year—one more reason for confinement when not supervised.

Other Beds

Cozy, cute, attractive, fancy dog beds are great, but save them for when your puppy is allowed (still supervised) in other rooms of the house and when he's reliably housetrained. Many dogs can boast of having a "bed in every room," but for now stick to the practical crate as Rufus's primary bed.

Food in the Crate

Feeding your puppy in his crate is not recommended because it turns many dogs into Guardians of the Supper Dish. This escalates to guarding everything in their crate, which only enforces unwanted aggressive behavior. (See Chapter 4, "Food, Exercise and Overall Care.")

Toy breeds can be trained to use a litter box (without the "privacy" cover that kitties prefer). A better choice for a dog is the litter box that contains specially treated pebbles rather than the conventional types of litter, which can create a sandstorm when the dog kicks with his back feet or when a long-coated dog shakes! Or, you can stick with paper training. Just watch where you drop the sports pages as you doze off.

chapter 6

What to Expect
from Your
Growing Pup

(Belgian Malinois)

As quickly as you can say, "*My puppy never did (or never would do) that,*" you can be certain your puppy will! The fun of watching a puppy grow up is best reflected in the store of memories every puppy owner has of his pup's silly antics, the results of curiosity and faltering attempts at being a big dog. As your puppy grows up, he leaves you with this legacy of warm, smiling memories, many of which may be somewhat catastrophic and only amusing in retrospect.

If you ever owned a puppy before, or know someone who has, you don't need to be reminded that new puppies begin life with a canine version of "the terrible twos." Unsupervised, a growing puppy makes a demolition derby of everything in its path! But that's the key—your key to preventing chaos: Supervision or Confinement.

Your care of the growing pup includes socializing him with other dogs and with people of all ages, preventing disaster, continuing education, remaining consistent in all you do and say, setting realistic goals, having great expectations and enjoying every minute of puppyhood that races by in a few months. A tall order? Yes, but together you and your smart, clever, wonderful puppy can do it!

Great Expectations

Many, perhaps most, pet owners today have to work. But too many go off to work in the morning expecting a young puppy that has already had eight to ten hours of sleep to spend the *next* eight to ten hours once again asleep while left alone. Expecting him to sleep or entertain himself in the confines of a crate for that long and to do it without relieving himself is expecting entirely too much of a young pup, or for that matter, of an adult dog.

Puppies will amuse themselves with toys, but you can't expect your pup to be perfectly behaved on her own for too long.
(Skye Terrier)

Obviously, it is unrealistic to think a puppy is going to sleep so many hours, although he will take short naps. But expecting adult bladder and bowel control in a young puppy is asking too much. (How many bathroom breaks do you take in an average eight- to ten-hour day?) Until fully grown, puppies nap a lot, play a lot, eat a lot—and eliminate often.

As the puppy matures, however, you can and should *expect* him to do the good things you've been teaching him: to walk nicely on a leash, to greet people by sitting, to come when he's called. Dogs, like children, generally rise to meet our expectations. There will be lapses—"selective hearing," teenage defiance, an occasional accident—but don't let down on your Great Expectations.

Two to Three Months

While some trainers feel that precisely seven weeks is the optimum age for puppies to go to their new homes in order to bond, more and more breeders are sending their pups out a bit later, or between eight and twelve weeks of age. This allows them to take advantage of learning first-hand what they need to know about being a dog from their mother and littermates. They learn to read body language, which is why your puppy watches everything you do or say and how you do or say it. They learn to respect a low warning growl or a sharp snap from Mom, which is why you can use that tone of voice as a warning, or the imitation snap "*aacht!*" to get the same results.

As for bonding, breed rescue groups nationwide place adult dogs every day with a high rate of success at having these dogs bond to their new owners. Earn your dog's respect and trust, and age will be no barrier to the bond that forms between you.

Mouthing Everything

Puppies are worse than babies at thinking everything (whether or not it fits) is meant to go into the mouth. In addition, they also learn first-hand about licking. The dam licks her infant puppies to stimulate and to clean them—their first lesson in being groomed. Licking at their dam's mouth is

---

A DOG'S SENSES

Sight: With their eyes located farther apart than ours, dogs can detect movement at a greater distance than we can, but they can't see as well up close. They can also see better in less light, but can't distinguish many colors.

Sound: Dogs can hear about four times better than we can, and they can hear high-pitched sounds especially well. Their ancestors, the wolves, howled to let other wolves know where they were; our dogs do the same, but they have a wider range of vocalizations, including barks, whimpers, moans and whines.

Smell: A dog's nose is his greatest sensory organ. His sense of smell is so great he can follow a trail that's weeks old, detect odors diluted to one-millionth the concentration we'd need to notice them, even sniff out a person under water!

Taste: Dogs have fewer taste buds than we do, so they're likelier to try anything—and usually do, which is why it's especially important for their owners to monitor their food intake. Dogs are omnivores, which means they eat meat as well as vegetable matter like grasses and weeds.

Touch: Dogs are social animals and love to be petted, groomed and played with.

both a submissive greeting and an appeal for food. Both domestic and wild female canids respond to lip-licking by regurgitating food for their young.

Some people like to be (what they call) kissed, but the majority do not appreciate all that licking! If you don't want your fully grown dog constantly licking at your hands and face, right now is the time to stop it. Create an unpleasant association by spraying a small amount of Bitter Apple on the back of your hand. As the pup approaches, offer the back of your hand and Rufus will go away with a bad taste in his mouth. (Remember to wash it off or you may be the next unwary victim.) No need to scold or punish. Let him learn the lesson all by himself. And don't give up after two or three tries; it may take several weeks to curb the lick habit.

Biting

Another form of mouthing that is learned in the cradle, so to speak, is actual biting. Puppies mouth—and bite—each other in play. They may also experiment on their dam's ear or tail. What they get if they bite too hard is an "*aacht!*" combined with a hard and speedy bite back!

Your puppy will watch everything you do to learn your body language. (Weimaraner)

Puppies *must* learn to inhibit their tendency to bite. When your puppy tests his teeth on your hand, be quick to let him know it is not acceptable. Scream, squeal or growl to let the pup know he hurt you, then stand up, move away and ignore him. "*If you bite, I won't play*" is understood by puppies, especially one that had the opportunity to learn it from his or her littermates.

Another method is distraction. The pup is mouthing your hand and suddenly bites. Give him an "*aacht!*" and put a toy in his mouth, preferably a rope, towel or other chew toy he can get his teeth into (i.e., not a hard bone). It's not the time for chasing a ball. You want to make the connection between what his mouth *was* doing and what it *should be* doing. It is difficult to keep at your fingertips all the things you need for teaching, but a small rope toy and a couple of treats will cover most situations.

A pup that has trouble learning to inhibit his bites may need to receive one sharp rap with two fingers on the top of the muzzle and a scowling, *"No bite!"* That's *one* rap with only *two* fingers—he's still a puppy, remember. It is the only time and the only form of physical punishment that is permissible. Then walk away and ignore him. This is not the puppy to play rough games with until he has learned to mind his mouth.

Puppies mouth and bite each other in play; you have to teach them they can't bite you! (Curly Coated Retrievers)

Fear Periods

Even the giant breeds go through fear phases when they're afraid of almost anything and everything from the dishwasher's rinse cycle to Johnny in his new Little League cap. It's part of growing up. Treated casually, it soon disappears.

Each dog is an individual, but usually one fear period surfaces sometime around the age of five to seven weeks. But don't be too surprised if your pup hits this stage at ten weeks or never goes through it at all. The puppy that suddenly won't step off the familiar curb is not being stubborn or defiant or stupid. He is fearful. So instead of forcing him to step off the curb he suddenly finds terrifying by jerking or dragging him by the leash, use a cheery voice and an enticing treat. (You see? All puppy owners soon get used to having small treats in every pocket! And to always wearing clothes with pockets.) For other types of fear demonstrations, use distractions such as tossing a toy or calling the pup to chase you.

Responding to Your Puppy

It especially bothers puppy owners and their friends when Rufus refuses to say hello. Yesterday you were teaching him not to bounce up on everyone, and today he's hiding behind your feet or under the bed! Pay no attention to this change. Ask friends to ignore him even when he is finally brave enough to crawl out to join the group, and also to remain still and silent, not to reach out to touch the pup or speak to him. Let Rufus sniff, and if he cozies up, that's fine, but don't be surprised if he darts away again. In a few days it will be history—that is, until the next fear phase.

If you coddle the puppy during a fear period, he may get stuck in that phase and forever be terrified of your guests, thunder, steps or whatever. A "fear phase" is a normal rite of passage. It can occur again at around five months and one more time between ten and fifteen months (before or after the teenage-adolescent stage). This is *not* the moment to introduce a pup to new people, places or things. If you recognize a fear phase, just play it cool for a week or so.

Large breeds, especially, go through an awkward stage at about three months of age. (Otterhounds)

Trying to comfort a dog's fear only makes matters worse, because your words and tone of voice are misunderstood by the dog to be your *approval* of his being afraid! Noise fear is overcome with a little chit-chat, a distracting game or toy and a cheerful, unconcerned attitude on your part.

57

Your puppy is taking in every minuscule part of your reactions. It's the old follow-the-leader ploy. If whatever it is doesn't frighten *you*, then Rufus will soon learn to trust your good judgment and follow your lead. Almost everything he learns from you is based on trust, so your primary goal is to be consistently trustworthy.

Thunder

Puppies in a teething stage need to chew, so make sure you have something appropriate available to chew on. (English Springer Spaniel)

A word about thunder. The majority of dogs are apprehensive to some extent when they hear thunder. Thunder is a *natural* occurrence and dogs are animals with many *natural* instincts. The sound of thunder is a warning to take cover, which is why many dogs head for a closet or underneath a bed. A crate-trained dog will head for that safe den. Just don't make the mistake of feeding the fear. Be cool.

Up to Twelve Weeks

By twelve weeks of age puppies have learned the basics of just about everything they need to know. Or at least, *they* think they have. Now it's up to you to direct and focus that puppy knowledge. What a puppy is *capable* of doing is not necessarily what you *want* the puppy to do. Not by a long shot!

Body-wise, the small breeds seem to have everything pretty much under control, but in large breeds, four to five months is the stage of the "ganglies." Legs are too long; feet don't always go in the right direction; an attempted jump at a toy ends in a pratfall. Stairs are major obstacles, resulting in a frantic scramble—going up or down. This is not the time for strenuous exercise or activity. He will soon outgrow this awkward stage. More memories.

Cute or Con Artist?

At this age, too, personality traits begin to emerge. You may suddenly notice you have an affable bully, a playful clown, an incorrigible con artist, an adoring slave or a bashful sweetie. These are individual *personality differences*. Temperament problems at this tender age are seldom spotted by pet owners, which may be just one reason they can become firmly established and increasingly difficult to cure. If you have a problem you can't solve, the quicker you seek professional help, the easier it will be to unravel.

Getting Aggressive

For example, aggression may surface as fear-biting where the pup dashes out from his crate (or behind the owner) to nip a person or other dog, and instantly retreat. This has nothing to do with the fear discussed previously. It is a form of aggression. Any form of real aggression—growling, snarling, snapping, biting—requires immediate professional help. It won't go away

Curious puppies can become real mischief-makers. (Curly Coated Retriever)

if you ignore it, and it can escalate quickly. This is not the same as a pushy or dominant but good-natured pup that can be readily brought into line. The latter is a personality type many pet owners prefer.

Let's say Rufus grabs a sock and runs under the bed with you in hot pursuit (probably with an irate vocal accompaniment). You get down on your hands and knees and reach for the sock. Aha! Now you are on *his* level, so he challenges with a warning growl: *"This is MY sock. I, Rufus the Great, stole it. Go get your own."* You cannot force him to give up the sock without a good chance of being bitten, so you retreat.

He has won without half trying, and by winning the first time he growls, the puppy has taught himself how

59

he can control *you*—and believe me, he will try it again. This proceeds predictably from a warning growl to snarling, snapping and finally attack biting.

It is vital that you end it now while he's still a puppy and, despite testing you in this way, he's still ready for you to be in charge. Aggression only feeds on aggression, so don't chase and don't get down on his level. Never mind getting the sock for now. Draw the puppy out by rolling a ball or any toy or treat alongside his hiding place, even pretending to run after it yourself. When he has the toy in his mouth, lure him to his crate or confined area. *No punishment.* Then return to retrieve the stolen object.

Kids need to be taught to pick up puppies correctly, supporting their hind legs. (Border Collie)

Submissive Urination

Another behavior that will become an ongoing problem unless properly handled is submissive urination, where the pup rolls over, exposes its vulnerable underbelly and wets. It occurs more frequently in bitches than in males, and is commonly found in certain breeds, such as Cocker Spaniels. This is not intentional urinating, but is a dog's way of yielding to a superior authority. Therefore, it is never a punishable offense.

Avoid anything the pup can perceive as dominance, such as standing above her or reaching down a hand to pet her. Crouch to her level with your arms next to your body. Let her come to you. Do everything you can to prevent activating a submissive response. This is the pup that will do well with lots of ignoring—and everyone knows how hard it is to ignore an adorable little puppy!

Being Nosy

This is the age of constant curiosity, and for the majority of puppies, curiosity is kept in check by an equally natural sense of caution. It's self-preservation at work. The pup will slink like a cat toward his first encounter with anything from a fallen leaf to a silent vacuum cleaner. He has to meet each challenge in his own way in order to build self-confidence. It will go on to become a form of play. Don't interfere unless it's a life-threatening situation. Intense curiosity about a supposedly empty antifreeze container calls for immediate interference!

This is also prime time for mischief. You can expect toilet paper streamers (it doesn't only happen in TV commercials); underwear in the living room; a bathmat, towel or baseball mitt tucked at the back of the crate. Rufus isn't being bad, he's having fun. Puppy fun. Reinforce your watch on all medications, household cleaners, garden plants and pesticides, everything you keep in the garage. If the puppy is around, don't put anything down for a second that could be harmful to Rufus (or the object) if he were to run off with it.

Taking your puppy to new places is a great learning experience for him. (Rottweiler)

Even a contentedly confined pup, if he is not given enough exercise, may occasionally go stir-crazy and strip the wallpaper, remodel the kitchen cabinets or dig peepholes in a hollow wooden door. However, the pup that is *not* confined, one that has been "so good" (for all of two days!) that you gave him "freedom" of the house—that pup has been given the opportunity to trash your antiques, soil every rug or carpet you own, tear down the curtains and leave you wondering why in the world you ever wanted a puppy in the first place. Confinement is a kindness. To both of you.

To Soothe Teething

At about four months of age the puppy teeth fall out as permanent teeth erupt, and with them comes the most intense period of chewing. Rawhides and hard indestructible toys are only part of the solution. To soothe those sore, itchy gums, dampen and chill a knotted piece of toweling (an old hand towel is good) and give it to the teething pup as a toy. He'll enjoy the massaging effect of chewing into the terrycloth and the cold will help those itchy, possibly painful gums. It's a good time, too, for fuzzy toys.

Playtime is serious funtime for puppies, who can make up all kinds of games. (Australian Cattle Dogs)

Don't try to play dentist; the teeth will come out by themselves. But check their progress when you brush the puppy's teeth. You should be looking for retention of baby teeth, with the permanent teeth erupting in front of or behind the first ones. Or for anything that appears to be out of line.

It is sometimes very easy to correct a puppy's dental problems—*if* caught immediately. A day or two can make the difference. It is quite common for the canines (fangs) not to meet, or to grow too long, allowing them either to jab into the roof of the mouth or into the lower gums. They need only be trimmed (or perhaps pulled if they are about ready to come out) in order to correct the situation. A puppy may bite or snap when you handle his mouth due to the pain of this malocclusion.

All dogs chew (and bark, and wag their tails), but a teething puppy *needs* to chew. If you don't provide the right toys, the pup will satisfy his needs on chair and table legs, doors, rugs—you name it! The most dangerous of these undesirable chews are electric cords, especially those attached to toasters, coffeemakers, etc., which take only one good yank to come crashing down. You can't watch TV *and* watch Rufus every second, so smear or spray that cord with Bitter Apple— and for good measure, keep at least *one* eye on Rufus.

Puppies and Children

Puppies and children seem to be made for each other, but little kids need to learn the rules about their puppy. Let small children play on the floor or the ground with their puppy so they don't have to pick him up. However, because a small, soft, furry, cuddly pup is as irresistible to kids as to adults, it's a good idea to teach the kids *how* to pick up the puppy safely—safely for both the pup and the children.

Puppies consider children fun-loving littermates! (Labrador Retriever)

Begin by having them sit on the floor and scoop the puppy up into their laps with hands firmly (but gently!) around the pup's mid-section. No one should *ever* lift or pull a puppy or dog by the front legs. Dogs do not have the same shoulder rotation as people do and pulling on the front legs can do permanent damage.

Older children (and adults) pick up a puppy with both hands firmly, but gently, around the ribcage and slowly lift him to chest level, holding him firmly against the chest. Express elevator rides cause fright or nausea, so put the puppy down slowly, too, holding firmly until *all four* feet are on the ground before letting go. Puppies wiggle—sometimes frantically—and kids have to be taught the difference between "holding firmly" and squeezing!

It should be obvious that this is not something your toddler can manage. Toddlers drop or throw everything they pick up—including puppies. Put the emphasis on patting the puppy gently and be ready to impose effective punishment on the child for pinching or pulling the pup. Keep crawling babies, toddling toddlers and eating puppies completely separated!

Puppies love to dig, so having a sand pit where it's an allowable activity is a good idea. (Shetland Sheepdog)

An older child should be encouraged to help with the pup's food and water, as well as grooming and training, all according to his or her ability in these areas. Don't expect to have all promises of care-giving fulfilled. Even if the kids aren't very adept at it, they will learn to think of others and something about the responsibility of owning a puppy.

While there are many reasons why a dog bites a child, two that top the list are teasing and hurting. Children are often not aware that they are teasing the dog. They wave their hands (with or without a toy or treat) over the pup's head to make the puppy jump up. The child thinks they are playing, but the pup sees it differently. To Rufus, it's a chase and he's trying to catch the object—which he does with his needle-sharp teeth, causing Molly to scream that she has been bitten. Not so. What she has really been is "caught"—caught teasing the puppy!

Puppies will go after children's legs as they run for the same reason. Either the kids cool it, or call for a Time-Out. Rufus goes into his crate for his Time-Out.

Small children can hurt a puppy unintentionally (a toddler plops down on the sleeping pup, for instance, or stumbles on a paw). Or intentionally, to see what happens when the ear is pulled, the eye poked, the leg bent backward—all things a young child would do to a stuffed animal without consequences. Kids need to be taught kindness to all living creatures, beginning with their puppy.

Forming Good Habits

Puppies of this age should be kept off furniture for two long-term reasons. First, because chairs, couches and beds are for people. Dogs have their own, which are kept on the floor. Second, and just as important, because puppies are apt to make Superman leaps *off* furniture, which can permanently damage the growth plates in their legs, something that can't be seen until the deformity is visible months later.

For this reason, too, don't try to force reluctant young pups to go down steps. Teach Rufus how when he is physically ready for it. If you want to see how scary going down stairs can be for a little puppy, go to the top of the steps and get down on all fours and have a good look. Now see how safe *you'd* feel about going down!

Puppies get away with doing things that are totally unacceptable in an adult dog. It may be cute to have your little puppy pouncing at your knees when you come home, but when he's a full-grown 140-pound Newfoundland, he'll knock you flat! Teach the young puppy right from the get-go the good manners you will want in your adult dog, and remember that the word is "Off" (*not* "Get down").

Puppy's First Playtime

When the puppy's immunizations are effective, you can venture further afield than your own backyard. Short walks and playtime in different environments are good for exercise and for socializing. These excursions will also teach you to pick up after your dog! It's the law in some places, just plain responsible dog ownership everywhere else.

YOUR DOG'S "HUMAN" AGE AND LONGEVITY

There are several ways of comparing dog years to human ones, but here is a modern one: One dog year equals fifteen human; two dog years equals twenty-four human. Then add four years to the human's for every one of the dog's (three equals twenty-eight, four equals thirty-two, five equals thirty-six, etc.).

Another factor regarding age is size. Small dogs live longer (eighteen to twenty years is not uncommon) and giant breeds (Great Danes, Irish Wolfhounds) live only five to ten years.

Play on a beach or a stroll in the park will be full of learning experiences for a young puppy. The retractable leash is perfect for these play-walks because it expands to give the puppy about sixteen feet of controlled freedom.

Fifteen to twenty minutes total time is enough at first, adding a few more minutes every few days depending on the pup (get home before he is tired), but also on the weather. Hazy, hot and humid is not the time for outdoor exercise. Icy pavements or streets may contain chemical melting agents, which must be washed off as soon as you get home. Take full advantage of time away from home to continue teaching your puppy. "Watch me" and "Wait" and "Leave it," as well as "Get it" and "Give it," can be easily taught now as part of a fun walk.

Five to Six Months

This is a great stage! Rufus has accepted most of your house rules. (All? He's a genius! None? What are *you* doing wrong?) He's big enough to go for longer walks and play more interactive games. The only things to cope with are the possible return of a fear phase and the onset of sexual maturity.

At five or six months (but sometimes as late as ten months), males will begin to lift a leg to urinate, and so begins the routine common to all male dogs of leaving a few drops of urine here, there and everywhere, often followed by kicking at the ground with the hind feet. It's called "marking territory," and it serves a definite purpose in the wild, a minor purpose on a walk. It's the pup's way of saying, "I, Rufus the Great, was here."

We don't treat it so casually, however, when it occurs indoors, so anywhere in the house, stop it with a sharp "*aacht!*" No need to punish, because this is not urinating. It is natural male behavior that must be modified so it doesn't happen indoors whether you are home or not. Take that as a warning: It can become a "separation anxiety" problem if you don't stop it. Clean up the drips with an enzyme cleaner (sold in pet stores) that will actually *remove* the odor, not just cover it up. If you catch him more than twice at the same spot (refrigerators seem to get this preferential treatment), clean it up and then use a repellent.

At six to nine months gardening becomes a favorite occupation. (West Highland White Terrier)

If your puppy lifted his leg at ten weeks, it does not mean he is an exceptionally gifted little boy. He may be more agile than most, or just a show-off. The opposite (still squatting at a year) is not a sign of abnormality, but may be attributed to laziness or a lack of athletic ability to stand on three legs. Pups often lean the lifted leg on a fence or tree until they get the hang of it, by the way. More amusing memories.

Six to Nine Months

By six months most dogs have reached about three-quarters of their full maturity. However, that refers only to their *physical* accomplishment. Mental maturity will take longer.

Neutering a male pup or **spaying** a female at about six months of age, or before sexual maturity, not only accomplishes the obvious (the prevention of unwanted pups), but has additional benefits, one of which is to virtually eliminate the incidence of cancer most often seen in the reproductive organs. In most towns a neutered dog earns you a discount—every year—on the dog's license.

At this age gardening becomes a favorite occupation. The pup may watch you dig, cultivate or plant and says to himself, "I can do that!" and so he does. The companionship of a pup in the garden is not to be denied, so provide Rufus with a couple of his own toys, and continue to teach the boundaries of the garden beds. Choose a one-word signal that suits you, such as "Out" (pronounced "ow-wt" for emphasis).

The Teenager

Doesn't that say it all? At almost any time between six months and a year, adolescence strikes! Your adorable, cooperative, smart little puppy will eventually become a teenager and be his usual charming self one day, and a demanding, disobedient demon the next. This is when the puppy that "never" suddenly *does*! It may be stealing socks or food, or charging around the house like a wild beast with a tornado on his tail, then ending up panting by his water bowl with (you could swear) a smile on his face. Join the joke. These, too, will soon all be memories. Be your consistent, firm but good-natured self and you'll soon get through it. It may take more firmness, a few more Time-Outs, complete consistency, but keep your cool. Puppy will be an adult for the rest of his life.

Playtime

Playing is serious stuff. Your puppy doesn't stop learning because the two of you are playing with a ball. He is learning to get it and bring it back to you or, he soon discovers, the game ends. That all-important "trust" is never more evident. If you give him a squeaky toy and suddenly hear silence, Rufus has removed the squeaker and you have to remove the toy. One snatch attempt and you'll be nailed (it is *his* toy), so use "Give it" with an irresistible treat in one hand. Remember your manners—say, "Good dog."

Agility Puppies like nothing better than their own playground. An old tire on its side is to climb in, out and around. Any length of ladder flat on the ground teaches foot dexterity.

A carton open at both ends that's two, three or four feet long becomes a tunnel to run through or hide in. A huge beach ball or an indestructible Boomer Ball will make a soccer star out of any pup.

The Sandbox Set Some people go so far as to include a sandbox (or sand pit) where the dog is meant to dig to his heart's content. A cautionary note: This is a great idea, but it can backfire. A dog that had never thought about digging will be taught how. And he may not stick to the sand pit.

Tug-of-War A basic game that all puppies play when left to their own devices is tug-of-war. You can play a gentle game with your puppy with a couple of cautions. Tug-of-war with a puppy is never a test of strength or wills. It is give-and-take play, nothing more.

Keep the knotted towel or rope toy on the floor, or at most no higher than the level of the pup's chest. There will probably be low growls and throaty noises. That's okay, but don't let Rufus get carried away. It's a fun game, not a life-or-death competition. *You* decide when the game should end. Pick a moment when you have possession of the toy or can remove it gently. At first, be prepared to offer a tantalizing treat in exchange. Then just stand up, say "good dog" and walk away. When Rufus is good at "give it" or "drop it," you will regain the tug-of-war toy that way.

The primary caution is not to play tug-of-war games with a dog that is going through a period of biting or one that shows any indication of being snappy, snarly or has any other signs of aggression.

The Future   All this educational playtime pays off. It's the precurser for obedience training. When your puppy has graduated from Obedience 101 (and is now officially known as Rufus, C.D. [for Companion Dog]), you can go right on to novice agility just for fun or to earn more titles! Or you can choose to participate in any one of the many performance events that are springing up for almost every breed or type of dog.

Dogs are not natural swimmers, but once taught, most love the water. (English Springer Spaniel)

Doggy Paddle

Dogs are not born knowing how to swim. In fact, many hate having to go out in the rain, to say nothing of tolerating a bath. But if you have a pool or live by water, teaching your puppy to swim is a *must*. This is one of those "for six months of age or older" sports because younger puppies lack coordination and may panic (and you may, too). Puppies and adult dogs drown just as easily as any land animal.

First check to be sure there is a safe, easy way for the dog to get *out* of a pool or pond (not up a ladder or through two feet of boggy mud). Coax the puppy to walk in with you, or carry him to where his feet are just off the ground. Then with your arm around his body and your hand under his chest, gently lead him back to where his feet will touch. Do not let go. Guide him to the chosen exit and show him how to get to solid ground or navigate a ramp. Towel dry (most pups love that part). End of first lesson!

Each day extend swim time only as much as he is still enjoying it, or at least that he's not panic-stricken. Guard your dog as you would an eighteen-month-old baby! *Never* let him have access to a pool or pond unless an adult is not only with him, but is able to watch him. Kids mean well, but they should not be given total responsibility. When the dog is older (next summer, perhaps), he'll have enough savvy to go in with the kids. Provide shade, water and a towel for a poolside pup. Yes, there are indeed poolside cabanas for dogs!

chapter 7

Training Your
Puppy

(Bulldog)

You began training your puppy when you took him in your arms and said, "Yes! This one's for me!" All the way home he listened to every word you said and how you said it. And, as you carried or led him through the door into your home, you clearly indicated to your puppy one of two things: *Here you are, puppy, it's all yours!*; or, *Welcome puppy, to our home!* Either you turned him loose to fend for himself, or you began teaching him how to become part of the family.

All of which is another way of saying that training your puppy does not only refer to obedience classes with an instructor to guide you. Basic training does not wait until your puppy is six months old. It begins immediately. You are teaching the pup, intentionally or not, what he's allowed to do—and thereby he earns your smiles and sweet talk—and what he is definitely not allowed to do. A puppy is a sponge, and spends every waking moment soaking up his environment and figuring out how all of it relates to *him*. (Puppies, like kids, are very "me" oriented.) Every dog needs to know his exact place within his new family circle.

Puppies use the "self-teaching" method if no one tells them otherwise. A pup learns to read canine body language from his mother and littermates. He learns by doing and evaluating the consequences *as* he is doing it. Let's say Rufus bites a littermate's ear. The other pup screams and bites back. "Hmmm," thinks Rufus, "she didn't like that," and he may try it again to find out how hard a bite is okay. If his second bite is too hard, Mom gets into the act and pins Rufus to the floor by the neck, which is her way of saying, "Cut it out—*now*."

A puppy learns by the actions he takes with his mother and littermates. (Boxers)

Rufus gets the message that biting hard will not be tolerated. It is his first lesson in "bite inhibition." However, once is never enough and he will try it again. Puppies need consistent and constant reminders. Bite inhibition just happens to be one of the most important lessons to be learned.

Now it is your turn to act with prompt intervention. To be successful, your action must be the smallest correction necessary to end the undesirable behavior and to teach what is acceptable. Note that a "correction" does not necessarily mean punishment, and it does not merely stop the misconduct. A correction always ends by having the puppy do something—anything—for which you can say "good dog." Your motto will be: *Teach, don't punish.*

Day One: Touring the House

Begin as you mean to continue. Bring the puppy into the house and give him a complete tour *on a loose leash.* This is the pup's first introduction to whatever limitations you want to put on his future access to your possessions—your furniture, golf clubs, books, the kids' toy shelves.

This is not the right time for "no." (The puppy might begin to think that "no" is his name!) Instead, use a guttural "*aacht!*" combined with a very slight tug-and-release of the leash *as* he sniffs to warn him away from untouchables. He's new at this, but just saying, "Puppy!" in a happy voice may be enough to get him to look at you—"Good dog." Back to happy chatter as you move on.

All you are doing is letting him know by means of prevention (a growl sound he understands) what things he will have to avoid in the future. Let him sniff first because he'll remember the objects more by scent than by sight. He looks up at you and he is praised.

Think of it this way: "No!" means "Don't *do* that!" whereas "aacht!" means "Don't even *think* of doing it!" Chit-chat is natural and pleasurable to both of you; but in the beginning the puppy will only pick up on his name because everyone uses it in connection with things he finds pleasurable—play, food or praise. If you use the word "din-din" many times while fixing his meals, that word will stand out in the midst of a five-minute speech on nutrition as a clue to the observant pup that he's about to eat. The human-canine teaching language is based on short, simple words that are consistently applied to specific actions.

Important Early Lessons

This first guided tour teaches your puppy the layout of his new home, what it looks like, smells like, even feels like (rugs, carpets, tile, wood) and that some things are off limits even to adorable puppies. There is one more important lesson he is learning from this adventure: that *you* are his new Leader, the He- or She-Who-Must-Be-Obeyed. If you do not take on this role, the puppy will. Somebody's got to do it, and he'll fill the vacancy immediately! You may be familiar with the saying, "Lead, follow or get out of my way." Every dog is born knowing it and continues to live by it!

Toilet Time!

House tour is over! Now it's down to specifics. Show Rufus where his water bowl will always be. Let him investigate his crate. Then take him outside (still on leash) to the exact area where you want him to eliminate. Stand there until he does. (Patience. He's new at this.) Praise quietly *as* he goes, after which you can make the same kind of tour outside, with warnings about flower or vegetable beds, bushes or plants.

Or you may live in a city and by law (and responsible dog ownership) must curb Rufus. Go to the quietest no-parking spot you can find. If you remain on the sidewalk, he will naturally want to join you, so stand down in the street with him. It will take time, plus your casual, confident attitude, to get him used to the noise, the confusion and the speed and size of trucks and taxis. No outside walking tour at this time. Wait until his immunizations are complete, by which time he will also be more accepting of city life.

Note: If the original trip home from where you picked up Rufus took more than an hour, reverse the two "tours" to let the pup eliminate first.

Puppy's Place

Back in the house, confine the puppy to the room you have puppy-proofed so he can investigate his new quarters. Encourage the cooperation of young children to "watch the puppy," but don't rely on them completely. Older kids, too, have good intentions, and the first week they may be just about perfect, but they have other things to do like swim or soccer practice, overdue homework, etc.

Young puppies are quick, clumsy and curious and they can get underfoot in a flash. While there is an obvious difference in size between a ten-week-old Labrador Retriever and a Chihuahua of the same age, their mental development is about the same. One difference is the smaller the puppy, the greater its need for physical protection. Watch it! The puppy is bonding to you, so he'll stay as close to you as he can get; i.e, in front, beside or behind you, or prone across your feet so you won't leave without him. Watch out, too, for tails that can get caught in doors, and human failings such as a show of impatience or anger in your face or voice. Young puppies are super-sensitive to every kind of hurt.

New puppies are bonding to you, and will want to be as close as possible. (Australian Shepherd)

Teaching Basics

There are three basic training ingredients needed to turn your puppy into an intelligent, well-behaved, cooperative dog. They are: Confinement, Prevention and Consistency. (There are more, but this is the foundation.)

Confinement

INDOORS

By keeping the puppy in one safe room in your house you are doing more than just keeping him safe. Rufus is learning to respect the limits you set. He is learning that you come and go and he doesn't have to panic when he hears you pick up the car keys. He is taking in all he needs to know about his new home and doing it all from a safe vantage point—safe from his viewpoint and yours.

A puppy learns more quickly from hearing "Good dog!" For example, when he entertains himself by destroying your best running shoes and is greeted with "*Oh no! Bad dog! Why did you do that?*" and on and on, he has learned only that you are irrational and not to be trusted. He looked up to greet you and you went nuts! After all, he only chewed your shoes *because they were there!* Got it? Confinement = "Good dog."

"Freedom" Isn't A puppy given free run of the house is unable to put two and two together. He can't understand that when you corrected him for chewing the hall rug, you also meant the bedroom rug—and the bathmat, the bedspread, the sofa cushions, the telephone book and everything else in the inventory of things *you* happen to value. Just think of all the punishments your puppy

avoids when he is confined in a safe place. As far as the pup is concerned, "free run of the house" only means he is "free" to get into trouble and "free" to have people mad at him. That double standard is precisely what breaks down the very thing you need to establish—trust.

Show your pup the lay of the land—indoors and out. (Golden Retriever)

The place where you choose to confine your pup when you can't be on Puppy Patrol may be your kitchen (with pet gates in doorways) or an exercise pen set up in any room that has destruction-free flooring. For short-term confinement, use the puppy's crate. A radio left on a "lite" or classical music station helps prevent separation anxiety when you're out of the room, or the house. The music and occasional voices relax the puppy, and the pup that is relaxed doesn't resort to excessive barking.

OUTDOORS

Two things keep a dog safe: one is a **leash,** the other is a **fence.** As Rufus grows up, you'll want him to be outdoors part of the day. If you own your own property, you have a wide choice of fencing. When considering which kind, remember that dogs dig, climb, chew and bark. (They also play, wag their tails and let us know we're the best, which are the other reasons for the fence!)

Fencing Considerations If there is something enticing like kids playing ball, or a cat, on the other side of the fence, that is reason enough for a dog to try to dig under or jump over the barrier. (Or just stand there and bark.) And if there is no such entice-ment, some dogs will make up their own reasons and dig anyway. (Siberian Huskies rate high on the "digger" chart.)

For the non-diggers (there are some), consistent training and the use of a pet repellent spray is enough. For the rest, or if you have no desire to find out the hard way, you'll need a fence installed with a twelve-inch extension below ground level and/or a trench of crushed stone. A sand-box or digging pit tucked in a corner of the yard might be the answer (it's called "directional digging") or it might only encourage the dog to think all the world's a sandbox!

This destructive behavior could easily have been prevented if the pup was watched or confined. (Shetland Sheepdog)

Solid wood fencing, such as stockade, offers some degree of noise deflection if your neighbors object to barking. It also provides a visual barricade to deter Rufus from barking at the sight of people or cars passing by.

If you opt for the newer **electronic (invisible) fencing,** be aware that not all dogs can tolerate the stimulus and not all dogs can be taught to respect it. Terriers top the list of escapees because they have been bred specifically to withstand pain as well as to chase prey. They'll go after a squirrel, chipmunk or the neighbor's cat without any concern about being zapped, prodded or buzzed. Then, of course, they may decide not to return to be zapped when their adrenaline level is not as high.

Undesirable behavioral problems can result. Some dogs become aggressive when confronted with pain, in particular the vet's needle. Others develop agoraphobia, or an intense fear of going outside.

The danger to all dogs is that this unseen fencing does not protect your property, including your dog, from roaming dogs or any person (including dognappers) from coming onto your property. So your dog can easily be attacked or stolen. Likewise, you would be held liable if your neighbor's child or cat wanders onto your property and is attacked by your dog! However, if this type of containment is your preference, you'll have to wait until your puppy is older and over the fear phases before attempting the essential training.

Puppies need to be confined so they don't have the opportunity to get into trouble. (Gordon Setters)

The Dog Run Perhaps fencing is not an option because you rent your home. A free-standing dog run is the answer for those dark and stormy nights (and equally dark early mornings) when Rufus has to go out, but you'd rather stay inside, thank you! This style of dog run can be taken apart and go in the moving van when you move.

It can also be moved from a shady spot in summer to a spot right by the back door for winter. Wire tops are available to keep Super Dog from climbing out, as are awning-type tops to keep out rain, sun or snow. A run can be set up on grass, concrete or a bed of crushed stone. Drawbacks? Only one. It is not meant to provide real physical exercise. Rufus will still need to be played with and walked.

Leaving Your Dog Outdoors Some breeds in some parts of the country will be kept outside all day while the owners are at work. There's no problem with it so long as the dog is *never* left tied up, which is cruel, unsafe and causes undue stress. A secure dog run with an all-weather dog house, an adequate fresh water supply and an appropriate variety of toys will cover part of the answer. The other important part is for the first person home to bring Rufus indoors to be with the family. Dogs are social animals. They need to be with people and to be part of the action.

Apartment-dwellers have no choice but to walk their dogs (after the series of puppy shots is complete) on sidewalks and in parks, which is fine by Rufus.

Your puppy has to understand you to obey you, so make sure it wasn't you who made the mistake. (Great Dane)

Prevention

Prevention is the easiest, quickest and surest way to discipline (teach) your puppy. Invariably, the mischief (or, if left for more than a few minutes, full-blown destruction) that your puppy got into will be discovered by you long *after* the fact. The pup that managed to chew through the leg of the coffee table obviously had not been watched for some time.

When you finally spot the damage, you do the normal thing: You blow up! Just please don't blow up at your puppy. Shout "NO!" only if Rufus is still hard at work. Whether caught in the act or not, give him a Time-Out in his crate. During his Time-Out, you can repeat ten times: *"I could have prevented that."* You can't undo the damage, but you don't have to let it happen again. Be fair to yourself and to your puppy, who doesn't know antique cherry in the dining room from a fallen branch under a tree. Wood is wood.

If you're going to let your puppy out without a leash, make sure it's in a fenced-in area. (Doberman Pinscher)

Here are the rules for **Puppy Punishment Prevention:**

When you can't watch, *crate.*

When you can't watch or crate (longer periods of time), *confine.*

When Rufus is "free" with you in the house, *watch*!

No one is perfect. No puppy is perfect. There will be mishaps, but follow the rules and there won't be total disasters.

Consistency

Your puppy hasn't even learned his own "language" and you're teaching him a foreign one, so you must be consistent. Use exactly the same word to mean exactly the same thing every time to enable the puppy to make a clear connection between the word and the desired action. Pretend he speaks a rare oriental dialect—you can't *punish* him for not understanding what you said!

Here's the standard example of how this works using the word "off." You'll be using it as a one-word command, which your pup will learn easily if you are consistent and don't confuse him. Use the one word "Off" when you mean *Don't jump up on Aunt Martha.* Also when you mean *Get off the couch, stupid.* And it can mean *Don't put your paws on the windowsill.* But it is a *one-word* command. Your puppy will be confused (*not* disobedient) if you say, "Don't jump up," one time, "Get off" another, "Get down" on another occasion and "Stay off" still another.

No matter what it is you want your pup to learn, remember, you're the teacher. (Wirehaired Pointing Griffon)

Looking ahead, how will Rufus know what you want him to do when you are trying to teach the commands "down" and "stay," which have nothing to do with "off"? All you have taught him is that sometimes you don't know what you're talking about! So, it is *one* word for each action. When you want to convey clearly to Rufus any form of "remove yourself," the word to use is *OFF.*

Think how quickly your puppy learned his name. That's because it is "one word" and you use it consistently. Okay, so sometimes you add a few endearing adjectives, but mostly, it's "Rufus" this and "Rufus" that. Get into the habit of using one-word commands consistently and Rufus will be speaking your language in no time.

Consistency is everything in the life of a dog. Older dogs can adjust when we change routines, but puppies thrive on knowing what to expect and when to expect it. Consistency makes you a reliable, trustworthy person. Trust is of prime importance to your puppy. If he trusts you, he will listen and learn from you.

What Your Puppy Learns

From three to six months the puppy is learning *how* to learn, so training sessions are tied in with fun, simply paying attention, praise and being with you. Discipline instills *self*-discipline and *self*-confidence, but puppies this age are still emotionally immature and most are sensitive to correction. Some will remain that way. Never make a harsh correction or punishment by hand, voice or leash. (Remember the oriental dialect barrier: Make yourself clear; don't punish him for not understandng what you said!)

Obedience instructors generally stick to the six months age minimum for beginners based on the probability that the puppy is housetrained (most training facilities are indoors and rented), on the puppy's ability to concentrate for more than two minutes, and on the owner's capability of handling a slightly more mature, less rambunctious dog. In other words, the "six months or older" rule prevents chaos in the average canine classroom.

Nursery School Begins

At three to five months of age all puppies are more or less equal in everything but size, and that difference isn't a problem to the pups. That is why **Kindergarten Puppy Training** (KPT) works so well. All the pupils have the same very short attention spans, some are a bit shy, some more bold, but all are curious and so respond favorably to new people, places and pups. Those that don't happen to fit into all those molds soon learn there's nothing to fear and most of it is fun. For the puppies, it closely resembles being back in the security of the litter.

KPT offers you instruction in basic grooming techniques and use of the collar and leash; if you happen to know all that, the socialization of your puppy is the best reason to attend.

A puppy that was in a litter of one or two, or a puppy that was taken from its littermates too soon, needs to be reminded how to behave around dogs. All of them learn how to interact safely with other pups, how to greet each other, how to play, how to "read" canine body language, how to respond to their own name and to their own special person and how to greet the strangers who belong to those other puppies.

The "graduates" then go on to pre-Beginner or Beginner obedience classes at six months of age, or after a short break. But that doesn't mean you should wait even one day. There may not be KPT classes where you live. The puppy eight to twelve weeks of age is ideally ready to learn, and the "adorable new puppy" syndrome is at its height! Besides which, everything the puppy can be taught earns the owner the right to brag! (Moms and dads have nothing on new puppy owners!)

"Off" is the command to use when your puppy jumps up on you. (Doberman Pinscher)

At-Home Training

An obedient, loving, fun companion is not difficult to achieve through home training. If you're after high scores in official obedience trials, then stick with the professional instructors who know and can teach you to recognize all the ways to achieve the perfection needed to make Rufus an OTCh, which stands for Obedience Trial Champion. But you can do all that later. In the meantime, you're the teacher.

What Every Dog Needs to Know

There are six standard commands: Heel, Come, Sit, Stand, Stay and Down. With a new puppy, it doesn't matter too much where you begin. The important thing is to practice any old time every day and never to be in any hurry to go to the next lesson. You do not set the pace for learning, Rufus does.

Training sessions should last only two to five minutes, which is approximately the length of your pup's attention span. If you push him longer than that, he will stop paying attention to you. This is FUN stuff! (You may also need to repeat that ten times to remind yourself occasionally.) End every session with a near-perfect performance. That could be one two-second sit, or three little "heeling" steps next to you. Tell him how "perfect" it was. Lay it on him! *Really* let him know how pleased you are he got it right.

Don't start a training session immediately after the pup has eaten because he'll be sleepy and those treat rewards won't be as enticing. However, you can practice at any odd time throughout the day, even if it is a three-second "stay." Your pup will love the attention.

Treats   Motivation for a puppy to do anything at all lies first in his desire to please you. Realistically, treats run a close second. Dog biscuits do not make good training treats because they take too long to chew. Tiny bits of plain cheese are the perfect taste-treat. A thin slice of hot dog will perk up the interest of almost any dog that's not concentrating.

Rewards come in three forms: treats, pats and verbal praise. To grade your "student's" qualification for a reward, consider a treat the equivalent of an "A," a pat a "B," and verbal praise a "C." Any two together equal an A+, so be very careful not to go overboard or you'll run out of appropriate compensation and the pup will quit!

Rewards come as treats, pats and verbal praise. Puppies love them all. (Mixed Breed)

Verbal praise has a range from *ecstatic* (for the first few correct responses from a very young pup) to a *calm* "good dog" as Rufus grows up and becomes more expert. *Don't* overuse cheese or hot dog treats when practicing. As each word command is fully learned, gradually cut back on the treats and substitute "good dog" or just a big smile. (An "A+" will retain its impact all the way through college, as will "ecstatic.")

Dog Talk

What you say to a puppy and how you say it can determine how quickly he learns. All conversation is perceived by the dog as meaningless sound. Try this: In the midst of some long-winded chit-chat, say his name emphatically and watch him take notice. When using the one-word training commands, remember that lesson. His name gives you his attention; one word tells him what to do. It is "Rufus, SIT"—loud and clear. Never, "Rufus, Sit. Sit. Sit. Rufus, you're not listening—I said Sit. *SIT, Rufus!*" That is called *nagging,* and Rufus will tune you out. The puppy is not being disobedient or stubborn. He's just confused—totally! Avoid sounding like a drill sergeant! Smile, speak clearly and let the dog do the barking!

Heeling

Heeling is not the same as going for a walk. No smelling the flowers, no lifting a leg on every hydrant. Heeling is an obedience exercise in which the dog stays close beside you, paying attention only to you and where you are going.

As your puppy grows up, heeling will become the safe way for you to walk your dog through crowds and across streets, ignoring all normal or unusual distractions. It is the easiest lesson to begin with because you'll be taking your new puppy outside on leash to eliminate and you can practice three times on each trip—on your way out, after he relieves himself, and coming back inside.

This will not be the heeling exercise as done in obedience class, but more of a lesson in "pre-heeling" because you can begin off-lead anywhere that's safe, indoors or out. And instead of "Heel," use the friendlier "Let's go!"

Begin by getting the pup's attention *as* he's trotting along next to you, to make him conscious of what he is doing. Some pups will follow if you lean over, quietly clapping your hands in front of their nose; some like to hear cheerful chatter; others just want to go wherever you go. As you move along, you can add an occasional, "Rufus, watch me!" No doubt by now you've noticed that some one-word commands are actually two or three words. Just run them together and your puppy will catch on perfectly.

Do pre-heeling exercises to begin to teach your puppy to heel. It's important to get your pup's attention first. (Mixed Breed)

Hold his attention by walking just quickly enough to make the puppy want to keep up with you. If he's not paying attention, stop and begin again. *No correction.* It all begins with just one step in the right direction, followed by verbal praise. Following a treat that smells good may get him started, but if a young pup's attention is totally elsewhere, this is not the right moment for a lesson. A few minutes of playtime, followed by a drink of water, may put him back on track to try again. Or wait until next time.

Practicing

You can practice anywhere, anytime, on or off leash. *As* you notice Rufus walking next to you—from fridge to stove, across the room, etc.—take advantage of the opportunity to get in a speedy, "Let's go!—good dog."

Be realistic in what you expect of a puppy. A few steps on command earn a reward. A few more steps earn a reward. A week later Rufus is heeling nicely? Praise and quit practicing immediately! Practice again later.

Puppies arrive in the winter, too, when outside lessons are not possible. A long hallway or a basement is perfect for indoor training. No distractions, limited space so Rufus can't go too far wrong, and you're sure to have his attention because *you* are the most fascinating thing around.

Tell him what a good dog he is for sitting, then start working on the sit-stay. (Belgian Tervuren)

Add some right turns for variety and to be sure he's really paying attention. *As* you make the turn, bend over and clap your hands to keep him on course. Left turns are harder because *you* have more to do. Put your left foot in front of the pup to gently guide him into the turn. Careful, or you'll step on the pup and he won't think this game is very much fun! However, if your left foot happens to bump the puppy, or he plows into it, don't apologize. If he thinks it was his mistake, he'll learn to pay closer attention. Repeat the "Watch me" signal.

If at First You Don't Succeed . . .

If you don't get the desired result from this or any other lesson, you just didn't explain it in a way the pup could understand, so try again. And again. And again! (Come on! How are you doing with that rare oriental dialect?) Keep your sense of humor. Puppies learn by consistent, patient repetition. If the pup gives up trying and you physically put him in the desired position for any of these training exercises, it destroys his self-confidence and the pup will begin to wait for your intervention. Puppies also give up if their efforts always end in punishment. It's called *learned helplessness*. As much as possible, let the puppy perform on his own. If you ignore his errors and put the emphasis on his successes, Rufus will learn quickly.

Teaching "Sit"

The "sit" command is an easy way to have your puppy show off his good manners. Rufus can sit when Aunt Martha comes visiting, when you meet a friend (especially a small child) out walking, when you are preparing his dinner, when he has to wait for just about anything from a dog biscuit to his turn in the pool. It is also one of the easiest exercises to practice because you can ask him to sit when-

ever and wherever you like. A Sit is especially good for little everyday things, like having his leash attached.

Teach your puppy to sit at all different times and for all different things. (Kuvasz)

The command is "Rufus, *sit*." You may have noticed that all commands are preceded by the dog's name; that's to get his attention so he knows you aren't talking to Johnny or Mary. Puppies are proud to have a name. It's when they reach adolescence (the terrible teens) that they, like other teenagers we all know, pretend they don't hear you. Any time you see the puppy about to sit, quickly say, "*Sit*—good dog." If he is already sitting nicely give him a "good sit" reward.

The easiest way to teach a young pup to sit is to get his attention with a treat held in front and just above his nose to make him look up. Then slowly move the treat backward over his head. Because a dog wants to keep his eye on the goodie, his backside will have to drop to the floor. It takes a little practice (on your part, too) but it's a tried and true means of getting an unforced sit. *As* he assumes the position, give the command, "Rufus—*sit*" and hand out a tiny portion of the treat. That's motivational teaching. The puppy performs the desired action by himself.

The other way is to have the pup beside you (left side), hold a treat in front of him with your right hand, and gently press down on his hindquarters with your left hand. With a large pup, you could put your left arm around his hindquarters and with a gentle forward motion, bend his knees, forcing the sit. And, as you are coping with all that, brightly say, "Rufus, *sit.*" You were warned! The motivational sit is easier!

If you followed the first method, and Rufus is doing a prompt Sit every time you give the command, you will soon graduate to using just the hand signal—making the same upward motion with your hand, palm up as you did in raising the treat over his head—and the pup will do a very nice sit. Tricks or treats, anyone?

Release

When the puppy is learning each of the commands Sit, Down, Stand and Stay, it is important that you teach him how you will release him from remaining in that position forever. The usual release is a simple "Okay!" while clapping your hands to regain the dog's attention. (Even puppies like applause.) Now's the time to love him up and tell him how utterly fabulous he is.

Teaching "Sit-Stay"

Once the puppy is able to sit still for a few seconds *every* time you ask him to, you can begin to add "Stay." Stand almost toe-to-toe with the pup until he gets the idea that you mean he has to remain sitting until he hears the magic word, "Okay." Two or three seconds in the beginning is fine. When you reach twenty to thirty seconds, you can put him in a Sit-Stay and move one step away, adding to the distance between you *only* as Rufus is able to hold the Sit-Stay. The object is to have him obey you, not to see how long he can stay put. It may take weeks to work up to a thirty-second stay. Puppies are squirmy!

Teaching "Come"

Teaching a young puppy to come when called starts off perfectly. The puppy learns his name and that people use it when they want to give him something fabulous like dinner or a new toy, so he comes running. Well, he soon learns it isn't a perfect world. He may hear his name called for a detested nail trim or to come in from outdoors just when he's having fun or enjoying a nap.

The biggest, the *number one* mistake people make with this command is to say "Rufus, Come" when there is no possible way to enforce it. Remember consistency? The puppy only has to disobey a few times when he hears "Rufus, Come!" and you have *taught* him (and he has learned) that he has an option. He can come, or not. Never give him that choice. Only call "Come" if the puppy is on his way into your outstretched arms, or on leash so you can guide him toward you. That rule is in effect until your adult dog is "proofed" (tested by numerous and diverse distractions) at two years of age. And to be honest, with lots of dogs, it's a lifetime rule.

Remember to always make "Come" a positive experience for your puppy. (Shetland Sheepdog)

The second biggest mistake is to call the puppy to come to you in order to scold him. That's a people no-no. Children are guilty of doing this, so be sure they understand they must never do it to their puppy. If you catch Rufus being naughty, *you* go to *him*. If he was up to no good and you come upon the scene of the crime even one minute later, it's too late to scold or punish a dog. Just never say, "Rufus, Come" if you are angry. Your tone of voice will tell him *not* to come, not to come anywhere near you; you have set him up to disobey you.

So say "Rufus, Come" when he is happily trotting toward you, or when you have him on leash a few feet in front of you and can guide him to you if he is distracted. Until he is older and much better educated, call the puppy with just his name. When he responds and is racing toward you, *then* get in a "Rufus, *Come*— good dog" as quickly as you can say it.

Always use a happy voice, crouch down, open your arms wide, smile—and when Rufus is on his way, say "Come!" If you've been having trouble getting a prompt response, have a treat ready for the big reunion. Another way to encourage a puppy to come to you is to pretend to run the other way. As the pup comes after you, stop, turn and say, "Come!" (Smile, treat or pat.) It's the irresistible game of chase and puppies love it! Admittedly, you have to be somewhat agile.

"Come" is one of the primary safety signals, and therefore your goal must be 100 percent compliance. In any type of emergency involving you or your dog, you must be able to rely on A+ obedience for "Come" and "Stay." (Straight A's will do for responses to the other requests!)

Teaching "Leave It"

Before we get to the final elementary command (Stand), there is one more your puppy needs to learn for his own protection, and that's the safety command of "Leave it." You're out for a walk and puppy comes upon a roadkill or carelessly discarded garbage. For the sake of your pup's health, you command, "Leave it!" and you will need to enforce it with a quick snap-and-release of the leash.

If your pup doesn't hear (or understand) the "Leave-it" command, get his attention with "*aacht*!" followed by "Leave it." (That's one word, by the way.) This one is so important that at four to six months of age you can even use entrapment as a teaching tool. When the puppy can't see you do it, plant a piece of trash, maybe an empty cereal box, on the floor and stick around until the pup goes to investigate. *As* he goes to sniff it, shout "Leave it!" and *as* he retreats at the force of your voice, say "Good dog."

On your walks, you can use this command if the pup has ideas of tasting fungus or your neighbor's tulips, or at home if he has in mind to sample the goodies on the coffee table or help himself to the popcorn. It is an extremely versatile and useful command. It also has an amusing side effect. Many young puppies respond to the extreme urgency in your voice and not only "Leave it" but do an instant Down—flat on the ground!

Teaching "Leave it!" can be very useful! (Shetland Sheepdog and cat)

Teaching "Stand"

When you give a dog any command, you have automatically assumed a dominant role and put the dog into a submissive one. Standing is a somewhat dominant canine posture, whereas the Sit and the Down are submissive canine positions, so it is sometimes difficult to teach a naturally submissive puppy to Stand when told. Given the command "Stand," many dogs will obey, but quickly lower their tails, ears and head—all submissive body language. Be gentle and patient. A perfect puppy Stand has four feet on the ground (that's the hard part), but it's also nice to see the head up and the tail wagging. Don't worry if at first your puppy would rather be a clown than stand still. Eventually they all grow up.

Rufus is learning the word "Stay" which (fortunately in this case) sounds a little like "Stand." Whenever you catch him standing still, it can work to your advantage. The puppy may pause for a moment to figure out which one you said, giving you the perfect opportunity to reinforce it with a "good *stand.*"

However, puppies do not spend much time standing around, so you'll have to teach him, not just rely on trying to catch him in the act. One way is to walk him into a stand. When he's pretty good at heeling, slow down and as you come to a stop, bring your right hand in front of him (palm side toward his nose) *as* you say "Stand." Perform this hand signal gently or Rufus will think he's going to be zonked and he'll duck!

This puppy knows what "Down" means and can do it all by himself. (English Springer Spaniel)

Practice by taking one or two slow steps (without a "Let's go" command) followed by a "Stand" command. Getting that head held high and happy and the tail wagging calls for a treat poised for a moment with a "Watch me!" A couple of reasonable or good "stands" are followed by a rousing romp in the early days of training. Standing still is *very hard.*

Again, take advantage of every possible occasion to ask your puppy to Stand. If you've been asking him to Sit before putting his dinner on the floor, now you can alternate a Sit with a Stand—and offer a treat reward right out of the dinner bowl.

Use the Stand command to begin a brushing/grooming session, but release him after a few seconds. A "perfect stand" is only required of an adult dog for about a minute. Standing is necessary for at least part of his weekly grooming, but not standing at attention. In fact, during every grooming session you can make use of the Sit, the Stand and the Down. What a clever puppy!

Teaching "Down"

Now we're talking total submission! Down is as low as you can get, and it is difficult for some puppies to accept. What is called the "dominant down"—a forced positioning of the puppy on his side with your hand on his neck/shoulder area—is restraint, not teaching. If your puppy is off-the-wall rambunctious and you are losing control, the dominant down is one method of regaining it—but never in anger, always firmly but gently. The drawback is you can get yourself into a struggling wrestling match—and come out the loser. Placing your hands on the puppy's shoulders and calmly saying "Settle" is a preferable, less combat-

ive method. Remember the rule to let a dog perform the desired action by himself.

With Rufus doing a B+ Sit-Stay, hold a treat in the fingers of your right hand (let him sniff it or see it), run that hand in front of his nose, down and out toward your feet. Be prepared to use your left hand on his shoulders *only* if necessary

to guide him into the Down position, which is flat on his tummy with front legs flat out in front. Deliver the treat *and* a "Good *down!*"and release.

"Stand" is a difficult thing for a young puppy to learn, but eventually he'll get it. (Brittany)

When the puppy can do a Down all by himself in response to "Rufus, down," you can skip the treat intermittently, begin to add a "Stay" and gradually—very gradually—work up to a Down of one minute. As he matures, he'll be able to stay down for five minutes (or more if necessary), but even one minute is an eternity for an active pup, and you need to remain within a foot or two to start the exercise over again should he get up.

It can't be emphasized enough: Go slowly—one step at a time—in all puppy training. If he did it right the first time, chalk it up to beginner's luck (his and yours!). Without steady repetition, he will forget it just as quickly. It takes the patient, consistent practice of each part of an exercise for the pup to learn that he must do it *every* time you tell him. If you go too fast, you will only confuse him.

You can hide your puppy's favorite toy, then teach him to go "Find it!" (Boston Terrier)

Remember the rare oriental dialect? Pronounce each word distinctly. "Sit," "stand" and "stay" are easily blurred beyond the pup's recognition. Put the "t" in SITT. Emphasize the "t" and "a" in STTAAY and put the "a-n-d" in stAND. Make DOWN an upbeat word, not a growl (a broad smile helps).

Teaching "Drop It"

Use "Drop it" when you want the pup to let go of a stolen or dangerous object. "Give it" may sound too much like "leave it," which could be confusing. "Drop it" has another advantage—you can say it so it sounds more like a growl (*"drrr-oppit"*) which makes the command more emphatic.

Timing

One final bit of training advice. You may have noticed how often the word "as" appears in everything you do in teaching your new puppy. Your puppy connects his action with your word command only at the precise instant they come together. Timing is vital. *What* you say is only as effective as *when* you say it. When you give a puppy a command AS he just happens to do something on his own, your timing is perfect.

Tricks and Treats

When your puppy has learned some of these basic things, you can practice by turning it all into fun. For example, put the puppy in a Sit-Stay, back off a foot or two, show him a soft toy and toss it to him. Don't go for a **catch** that requires a Superman leap into the air. The idea is to have him actually catch it!

Put him in a Sit-Stay and let him watch you hide a toy under the edge of a nearby chair. Keep him on a stay for a moment more, perhaps as you wonder out loud "Where is Teddy?" Then give him the release and cue, "Okay—find Teddy!" If he hasn't figured out what to do, help him look for it, but let him **"find" it.**

Going back to the "*as*" routine, you can teach your puppy almost any trick that he can perform by himself simply by giving that action a one-word command. (Don't worry if it's actually two words.) Dogs like to **roll over** onto their backs and wriggle, especially on a nice thick rug! Turn this back-scratching into a trick by catching Rufus *as* he begins and saying, "Rufus, roll over. Good boy!"

As your puppy grows up, he'll understand more and more of your language and you'll be able to use phrases that have great impact as tricks. For example, instead of saying "roll over," say, "Rufus, can you do your *rollover* exercises?" to bring on a wriggling, leg-flailing routine that is worthy of applause. For starters, keep it simple.

When Rufus has reached the stage of being able to hold a steady Sit-Stay, you can add another trick. **Balance a small dog biscuit on top of his nose** *as* you say, "On trust." (You may have to hold his head steady the first few times.) When he has held it for a second or two, give him the release signal ("Okay" or

"Take it") *as* you gently but quickly lift his chin up, which will toss the biscuit into the air so he can catch the biscuit as it falls.

Kids and puppies love to play **hide-and-seek,** but anyone can get in on the game. Dogs seek by scent, so at least in the beginning crouch down to be nearer the pup's level. Put Rufus in a Sit-Stay, let him see you hide (behind a chair or a door), crouch down and then call out "Okay!" Be sure he finds you even if it means you have to call out his name a couple of times. Make a big deal of it when he does—and then repeat the game. Don't make it any more difficult until he can find you instantly at the first level.

Shaking hands is easy to teach, and is one of lots of games you can play with your puppy to have fun and spend time together. (Mixed Breed)

Reward him occasionally with a small treat, but make finding you the most exciting part of the game, which means you will progress slowly from hiding where he can at least partially see you, to hiding in another room and eventually the back of a clothes closet where your scent will be masked. He won't play if it isn't fun, so be sure he does find you every time.

Shaking hands is an old favorite and easy to teach— touch the toes and most pups will raise that paw. Lift it gently and say, "Shake hands" (or "Give me a paw") *as* he does. When that much has been mastered, you can turn it into a paw raised higher, and without shaking it, say, "Wave goodbye!" But that's for later; a polite puppy handshake is fine for now. The opposite of "Off" for jumping up is two paws raised in a jump-up greeting, *only* on a command of "High five!"

There are plenty of games to play outdoors—mostly chasing toys or navigating obstacles. The "puppy pen" can contain all kinds of things so long as they are safe to chew, close to the ground and can be kept relatively clean.

There are many breed-specific performance events that can be introduced at a puppy level. Contact breed clubs for information on puppy training. Lure coursing is fun for sighthounds (like Greyhounds and Whippets) and most other breeds. Fetching suitable objects on land or water is great for retrievers. Go-to-ground for all the small terrier breeds is easily accomplished using cartons opened at both ends to form a tunnel.

There's no such thing as failure in puppy games. Some dogs are naturally better than others at games in general. Some enjoy one type of game more than another. Go with your pup's game preferences now and you can expand them into tricks later. Don't be a pushy parent. Keep learning fun for both of you.

Your

Puppy's

part three

Health

8

Health Care

(German Wirehaired Pointer)

The purpose of this chapter is to help you keep your puppy healthy, so there will be no vivid descriptions of terrifying rare diseases to scare you out of your wits. Maintaining good health means being able to read the first signs of an impending health problem in order to take prompt action. A major part of canine health care today lies in prevention, which includes regular veterinary care, quality food and regular grooming.

It is sometimes easy to be mystified or confused by veterinary terms that may in fact refer to a mild canine ailment. The information you will find in these pages will *never*—even remotely—replace the need for your veterinarian! But it will let you become familiar with many of those terms as well as some of the more common canine health problems, which in turn will help you communicate with your puppy's doctor.

Know Your Puppy

As you watch your puppy in order to fend off pranks, mischief, destruction and disaster, you will also be observing what is normal for your particular puppy—what he usually looks like: eyes, mouth, ears, body posture, energy level; how he behaves or reacts; how much he eats and drinks (and eliminates) on a normal day-to-day basis. This casual observation will enable you to notice when something is wrong, when he's "just not himself" or has a runny nose, when he's limping slightly on one leg, and so on.

By carefully observing your pup—or puppies—you'll be able to tell when there's a problem. (Golden Retrievers)

As luck would have it, these things are invariably first noted late at night, usually at bedtime. In fact, Murphy's Law might state that the more of an emergency the situation is, the later at night it will occur. Bedtime for veterinarians, too! That's when you can check the information here, not—definitely *not*—to play doctor yourself, but to learn what might be wrong, what immediate action you can take, what to relay to the vet when you do call. Sometimes it's a relief just to

103

get an indication of how serious the problem is. Panic over a puppy's welfare is par for the course in raising a dog. But, for example, poison of any sort calls for *immediate* action regardless of the time of day or night. Vomiting once, due to a honey-bun you caught Rufus polishing off, can wait until morning.

Choosing a Veterinarian

Choosing a vet is difficult if you are new to pet owner-ship or if you've moved into a new area. One way to start is by asking friends and neighbors of their experiences with local veterinarians, keeping in mind what kind of pets they have and how their ideas of pet care coincide (or collide) with your own. That's one starting point.

Veterinary practices are no longer limited to a waiting room, examination room and surgery run by one person. Many today are in large complexes where all your pet's needs can be met under one roof—medical care, food/supplies/toys, grooming, boarding, train-ing and behavioral consultations. A veritable pet mall!

At the other end of the scale is the mobile vet who only makes house calls and arrives with an equipped surgery right in the van. What is more important to an increasing number of busy pet owners is the fact that the vet who makes house calls comes at the owner's convenience and confronts the pet in its own environment as a friend.

There are small animal hospitals with numerous doc-tors, and also the solitary vet set-up exchanging days off and holidays with a nearby doctor who has a similar practice.

Then there are animal emergency centers manned around the clock, year-round, often with a small quali-fied permanent staff and area veterinarians taking turns on duty, some paid, some performing a commu-nity service.

In other words, you have a lot to choose from—and having made a choice, you need never feel stuck with it. Feel free to call and ask if you may visit the offices. If the answer is "no," you wouldn't feel welcome with your dog in tow either. The perfect time to get to know a veterinarian and to establish the necessary confidence in the doctor, the staff and the way the office is run, is when taking care of those puppy shots. If you are not completely happy with your choice, as you become involved in the world of dogs— training classes, for example—you'll meet others with whom you can discuss other veterinarians.

You are the vital link between your dog and his doctor. The dog can't say what is bothering him or how he feels, so you must be able to communicate to the veterinarian how the dog's current actions (eating, eliminating, sleeping and general behavior) differ from what is normal for your particular dog. If you are unable to have such an open conversation, feel cut off, or sense hostility or impatience, go elsewhere.

On the other side of the coin, *you* have to listen to what the vet is saying, watch what he or she is showing you to do and follow instructions to the letter. Many a good doctor has to cope with a good dog whose owner just doesn't pay attention.

> **WHEN TO CALL THE VET**
>
> In any emergency situation, you should call your veterinarian immediately. You can make the difference in your dog's life by staying as calm as possible when you call and by giving the doctor or the assistant as much information as possible before you leave for the clinic. That way, the vet will be able to take immediate, specific action to remedy your dog's situation.
>
> Emergencies include acute abdominal pain, suspected poisoning, snakebite, burns, frostbite, shock, dehydration, abnormal vomiting or bleeding, and deep wounds. You are the best judge of your dog's health, as you live with and observe him every day. Don't hesitate to call your veterinarian if you suspect trouble.

Preventive Care

The easiest way to make sure your dog is well cared for is to establish a routine, then follow it every day.

For optimal health, your puppy needs high-quality dog food, fresh clean water, exercise and sleep (Chapter 4). He needs these every day, in varying amounts as he grows older. Beyond this basic care, **take the time, every day, to run your hands over your puppy**. You can do this while you're grooming him. But don't just pet and brush him; instead, run your fingers through and under the coat so you can feel the dog's skin. As you do this you will get to know the feel of your dog. Should he pick up a tick, you will feel it with your fingers. If he has a cut, a lump or bruise or a skin rash, you will feel it.

By checking the dog like this every day, you will find these things before they turn into bigger problems. When you start this routine in puppyhood, your dog will come to love it, and will be more accepting of being petted by other people—especially the veterinarian—as an adult.

The best time for this exam is after you have brushed your puppy. Start at his head and, using your fingertips to navigate through the fur, feel all over your puppy's head, including around his muzzle, eyes, ears and neck. Take your time and be gentle; think of it as giving your puppy a massage.

Continue working your hands down your puppy's body, examining his shoulders, back, sides, legs and tail. Run your hands down each leg, handling each toe on each paw, checking for burrs and foxtails, cuts and scratches. If you find any minor cuts and scrapes, you can wash them off with soap and water and apply a mild antibiotic ointment. However, if a cut is gaping or looks red and inflamed, call your veterinarian. Check your puppy's tummy, too. Fleas like to hide in the groin area and behind elbows—don't miss those spots.

Once you've gone over his entire body this way, return to his head. It's time to check your puppy's **mouth**, looking for inflamed gums, foreign objects or possible cracked or broken teeth. Become familiar with what the teeth look like, inside and out. This is a good time to brush the teeth.

Next, clean the inside of the **ears**, gently wiping them with cotton balls moistened with witch hazel or a commercial product made especially for cleaning the ears. As you wipe out the ear, check for scratches or foreign objects and give the ear a sniff. If there is quite a bit of discharge and the ear has a sour smell, call your veterinarian; your puppy may have an ear infection.

Check your puppy's **nails**. They need regular trimming, but not every day. However, a daily check will keep you posted on whether any nails are chipped or cracked.

Odds and Ends

A healthy puppy is active, alert and ready to go when awake, but because rapid growth is tiring, long naps are normal. Then there's the difference between a "nicely filled-out puppy" and one with a "big fat tummy." The latter (a swollen or distended stomach) is more likely to be caused by roundworms than by overeating.

Your Puppy's Temperature

The temperature of a healthy puppy ranges from 101 to 102.5 degrees Fahrenheit taken with a rectal thermometer. That information will keep you from freaking out when the vet casually says, "His temp is 102 degrees" and what pops into your head is the human norm of 98.6.

To take the pup's temperature yourself, shake down a rectal thermometer until it reads about 95, then put a dab of petroleum jelly on the tip and, holding the pup's tail with one hand (so he won't sit down) insert it gently with a slight twisting motion about one inch into the rectum. Hold it for at least a minute (three minutes is best, but that's a long time for a pup). Any reading over 103 degrees is cause for calling the veterinarian. It helps to know that puppies and small dogs have faster heartbeats than large dogs.

When to Call the Vet

Base your puppy's health on the rule of "better safe than sorry." If you are unsure of anything concerning the health of your puppy, call your veterinarian's office. If it's minor—something every puppy goes through—a certified technician on staff can probably help, either without bothering the doctor, or after briefing him on the problem. If the matter warrants veterinary examination and/or treatment, you'll be advised of that, too.

Always remember that your veterinarian is practicing *preventive medicine.* He needs your help in order to make it work for your puppy. Here are some typical problems that would warrant calling the veterinarian:

1. Diarrhea or vomiting that lasts more than one day. Call immediately if the contents of either one are dark or contain blood.

2. Complete loss of appetite for more than a day.

3. A fever above 103 degrees, or shivering in a warm room.

4. Seizure or convulsions.

5. Choking, coughing or raspy breath.

6. Any sudden change in water consumption, urination or general behavior that lasts for more than one day.

7. Limping that does not improve after one day of complete rest (crate confinement) or any lameness that is painful.

8. Runny nose, watery eyes, drooling or slobbering (from a dog that doesn't normally do either).

Immunization

Healthy puppies, in order to stay healthy, need to be immunized against several potentially lethal diseases. The vaccinations your puppy has had, and may be given in the next few weeks, are often referred to as "puppy shots" or "temporary immunizations," which might lead you to believe that the final shots in the series of these protective vaccines are "permanent." They are not!

An annual routine check-up by your veterinarian will include the administration of "booster shots," which are adult updates of puppy shots (plus whatever new protection has been made available through ongoing research). These are an essential part of keeping your dog healthy.

SCHEDULE OF PUPPY SHOTS

Breeders will generally have seen to it that their puppies have had their first set of shots, sometimes even the second depending upon the age at the time of sale. From then on it's up to the owner to follow a schedule set by the veterinarian. The complete series is usually given at eight, ten and twelve weeks of age.

These first immunizations, or puppy shots, are often given as one injection and include Distemper, Hepatitis, Leptospirosis, Parainfluenza and Parvovirus vaccine. Known simply (and gratefully!) as "DHLPP," it is first given at about eight weeks of age. The next shots may add "C" for Coronavirus if advisable in your area.

Infectious diseases include distemper, infectious hepatitis, leptospirosis, parvovirus, coronavirus, parainfluenza (kennel cough) and rabies.

Distemper Distemper is a very contagious viral disease that used to kill thousands of puppies. Today's vaccines are extremely effective, but puppies still die from it. If your puppy has an immune-system problem, or if he wasn't properly vaccinated, he could get distemper. Symptoms show as weakness and depression, a fever and a discharge from the eyes and nose. Infected puppies cough, vomit and have diarrhea. Intravenous fluids and antibiotics may help support an infected dog, but unfortunately, most die.

> **YOUR PUPPY'S VACCINES**
>
> Vaccines are given to prevent your dog from getting an infectious disease like canine distemper or rabies. Vaccines are the ultimate preventive medicine: they're given before your dog ever gets the disease so as to protect him from the disease. That's why it is necessary for your dog to be vaccinated routinely. Puppy vaccines start at eight weeks of age for the five-in-one DHLPP vaccine and are given every three to four weeks until the puppy is sixteen months old. Your veterinarian will put your puppy on a proper schedule and will remind you when to bring in your dog for shots.

Infectious Hepatitis This is a highly contagious virus that primarily attacks the liver but can also cause severe kidney damage. It is not related to the form of hepatitis that affects people. The virus is spread through contaminated saliva, mucus, urine or feces. Initial symptoms include depression, vomiting, abdominal pain, high fever and jaundice. Mild cases may be treated with intravenous fluids, antibiotics and even blood transfusions; however, the mortality rate is very high.

Leptospirosis Leptospirosis is a bacterial disease spread by the urine of infected wildlife. If your puppy drinks from a contaminated stream or sniffs at a bush that has been urinated on by an infected animal, he may pick up the bacteria. The bacteria attacks the kidneys, causing kidney failure. Symptoms include fever, loss of appetite, possible diarrhea and jaundice. Antibiotics can be used to treat the disease, but the outcome is usually not good, due to the serious kidney and liver damage caused by the bacteria. Leptospirosis is highly contagious; other dogs, animals and people are susceptible.

Parvovirus Parvovirus, or parvo as it is commonly known, attacks the inner lining of the intestines, causing bloody diarrhea that has a distinct odor. It is a terrible killer of puppies and is extremely contagious. In puppies under ten weeks of age, the virus also attacks the heart, causing death, often with no other symptoms. The virus moves rapidly and dehydration can lead to shock and death in a matter of hours.

Coronavirus As is implied by the name, this is also a virus. Coronavirus is rarely fatal to adult dogs, although it is frequently fatal to puppies. The symptoms include vomiting, loss of appetite and a yellowish, watery stool that might contain mucus or blood. The stools carry the shed virus, which is highly contagious.

Parainfluenza (Kennel Cough) This respiratory infection can be caused by any number of different viral or bacterial agents. These highly contagious, airborne agents can cause a variety of symptoms, including inflammation of the trachea, bronchi and lungs, as well as mild to severe coughing. Antibiotics may be prescribed to combat or prevent pneumonia and a cough suppressant may quiet the cough. Luckily, the disease is usually mild and many puppies recover quickly without any treatment at all.

Rabies   Rabies is a highly infectious virus usually carried by wildlife, especially bats, raccoons and skunks. Any warm-blooded animal, including humans, can be infected. The virus is transmitted through the saliva, through a bite or break in the skin. It then travels up to the brain and spinal cord and throughout the body.

Behavior changes are the first sign of the disease. Animals usually only seen at night will come out during the day; fearful or shy animals will become bold and aggressive or friendly and affectionate. As the virus spreads, the animal will have trouble swallowing and will drool or salivate excessively. Paralysis and convulsions follow.

Immunizations provide protection against these contagious diseases that can be (and usually are) fatal in young puppies, so the series is a very inexpensive form of health insurance. As a bonus, each time you take your puppy in for shots, the veterinarian will check the pup's general physical condition and growth, and answer your questions. Well worth the price of admission!

Kennel cough vaccine is given to young puppies only if there is a real danger of exposure. As its name implies, this immunization is a sensible requirement of well-run boarding kennels. The vaccine is administered as a nasal spray at least ten days prior to possible exposure.

Rabies and **Lyme disease** protection are routinely given to pups at six months of age in most parts of the United States. A year later, the rabies vaccine used will last three years.

Internal Parasites

Roundworm is a very common internal parasite in young puppies. Take a fresh stool sample on your first visit to the vet so it can be checked for worms. Roundworms are easy to treat, but can cause serious problems if left untreated. All these parasites are treatable after diagnosis, usually examination of your puppy's stools. Don't try it yourself because the "cure" is actually a poison to kill the worms that could harm your puppy if incorrectly administered.

Hookworm eggs burrow into the skin through a puppy's feet or are acquired by eating an infected animal's stools. In the body, hookworms migrate to the dog's small intestines, where they latch on and suck blood. When the worms detach and move, they leave open wounds behind, causing bloody diarrhea—the first sign of infection. People can get hookworm in infected soil, too.

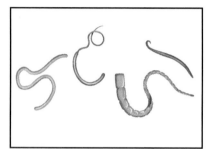

Common internal parasites (l-r): roundworm, whipworm, tapeworm and hookworm.

Whipworms feed on blood in the large intestine, and a heavy infestation leaves a puppy looking thin, usually with watery or bloody diarrhea. Whipworm eggs can live in soil for many years and can be acquired by eating new grass, digging up a bone or licking the dirt.

Tapeworms also grow in the dog's intestines, where they absorb nutrients from the intestinal wall. They're acquired by swallowing fleas, the intermediary host. You can tell if your dog has tapeworm by noticing white rice-like segments in its feces. These are the segments of growing tapeworms.

Heartworm infestation is passed on to the dog by a bite from a mosquito, which is the intermediary host between infected animals. The worm itself grows in the chambers of the heart and is almost always fatal. The treatment involves the use of arsenic to kill the heartworm, itself a dangerous procedure.

Heartworm preventative in the form of a pill is given every day or every thirty days, depending on which type you choose, but only *after* your veterinarian has obtained a negative result from a preliminary blood test that must be done annually. When the medication is started and how long it is continued depends on the incidence of heartworm in your area. In most of the

U.S. now it is administered year-round. The medication also controls hookworm, whipworm and roundworm, making it another excellent investment in your pup's good health.

Spay/Neuter

Myths abound on the subject of spaying (for females) and neutering (for males), but the facts are plain and simple: it is extremely beneficial to your pet's health. Either operation is performed when the pup is about six months of age, or just approaching sexual maturity, but discuss with your vet the best time for your puppy. It is a minor operation from which the pup recovers quickly. The major benefit is that you, as a responsible pet owner, will have eliminated any chance of adding to the overpopulation of unwanted puppies.

Spaying involves the removal of the uterus, tubes and ovaries. Your dog will *not* come into heat, or estrus, every six months and thus will *not* require three to four weeks of absolute confinement, which means *on leash* even in your own backyard (roaming males climb fences, leap tall buildings, etc.). Of course, it also means no stains on furniture or clothing. Spaying eliminates an estimated ninety-five percent of the most common cancers (mammary and uterine). And she will *not* become obese unless you overfeed her and don't provide her with sufficient exercise.

ADVANTAGES OF SPAY/NEUTER

The greatest advantage of spaying (for females) or neutering (for males) your dog is that you are guaranteed your dog will not produce puppies. There are too many puppies already available for too few homes. There are other advantages as well.

ADVANTAGES OF SPAYING

No messy heats.

No "suitors" howling at your windows or waiting in your yard.

Decreased incidences of pyometra (disease of the uterus) and breast cancer.

ADVANTAGES OF NEUTERING

Lessens male aggressive and territorial behaviors, but doesn't affect the dog's personality. Behaviors are often owner-induced, so neutering is not the only answer, but it is a good start.

Prevents the need to roam in search of bitches in season.

Decreased incidences of urogenital diseases.

Neutering, or the removal of both testicles in the male dog, not only eliminates unwanted offspring, but also diminishes the dog's desire to "mark" or urinate on

113

everything that stands upright. It even reduces the normally strong odor of male urine. It will *not* turn Rufus into a wimp, or change your dog's personality—except perhaps to calm aggressive outbursts when encountering other male dogs. He will still protect you and be as good a watchdog as ever. Neutering will *not* cause him to get fat. Overfeeding and under-exercising, however, will.

In fact, some of those myths came about because dog owners were told (and wanted desperately to believe) that behavior problems would change for the better or all disappear after neutering the dog. Sorry, folks! Only certain sex-related behaviors change. Changing undesirable behavior is up to you—with help from your obedience trainer or a behaviorist.

Skin Ailments

Allergies Dogs' allergies are primarily caused by ingestion or inhalation of such things as grasses, weeds and pollen (or caused by foods, with reactions to wheat or beef common). Contact allergies are less common but can be caused by something as innocuous as man-made fiber rugs or dog bedding. A change to pure cotton or wool is the simple solution. Mild skin irritations are often controlled by special shampoos.

Once the allergen has been detected, the "cure" may be simply to avoid the culprit, as, for example, in the case of a reaction to wheat or beef. More complex cases require veterinary testing and antigen shots over a long period of time. This is the same desensitizing treatment people receive and,

To keep fleas off your dog—and out of your house—you'll have to treat your pet and your home. Make sure you check your dog after every excursion in the great outdoors. (Briard)

like the human treatment, can be costly and time-consuming.

Hot spots are intensely itchy spots on the skin that worsen as the dog licks or scratches them. The most common cause is a flea bite. If you catch it when the spot is small, clean it with an antibiotic spray and spread a repellent such as Bitter Apple on the surrounding hair to keep the dog from irritating it. Work hard on getting rid of the fleas. If the area is large when you discover it, consult your veterinarian. It may be more than just a hot spot.

Ringworm is not a worm at all, but a fungus that grows under the skin in a circle with loss of hair in the center. This is a highly contagious disease that can be transmitted both ways—from dogs to people or people to dogs. Caught early enough, you can treat it yourself with Tinactin (from the drugstore), but keep the kids away from the dog until the cure is complete.

Fleas

Fleas are a prolific, common environmental enemy of people and animals. Despite the number of products on the market to rid the dog, the house and the garden of this pest, the flea continues to thrive.

The first thing to do is accept the fact that if you discover one flea on your pet, your house probably contains thousands of fleas in various stages of growth. Treating the dog will make him more comfortable temporarily, and spraying him with one of the new insect growth regulators 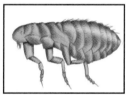 will inhibit further growth of eggs or larvae on the dog or when they drop off onto your carpet. However, the very first thing to do is clean your house.

The flea is a die-hard pest.

TREATING THE HOUSE

Remove birds and all small animals (dogs, cats, gerbils, etc.) and cover aquarium tanks. Put away all food and dishes (pets' and people's). Send the kids off fishing with grandpa. Vacuum every carpet, every rug, every crevice in the floors and baseboards of your house. Close the windows and turn off the air-conditioner. Then set off a sufficient number of foggers containing insect growth regulators (IGRs) to do the job. Follow directions carefully, and plan for all pets and people to be out of the house for five hours or longer.

FIGHTING FLEAS

Remember, the fleas you see on your dog are only part of the problem—the smallest part! To rid your dog and home of fleas, you need to treat your dog *and* your home. Here's how:

• Identify where your pet(s) sleep. These are "hot spots."

• Clean your pets' bedding regularly by vacuuming and washing.

• Spray "hot spots" with a nontoxic, long-lasting flea larvicide.

• Treat outdoor "hot spots" with insecticide.

• Kill eggs on pets with a product containing insect growth regulators (IGRs).

• Kill fleas on pets per your veterinarian's recommendation.

TREATING THE DOG

Shampoo, then dip or spray the dog. Since you all have to be out of the house, this would be a good time to send Rufus to the groomer's for a flea shampoo and dip or spray. Or do it yourself. (A warning if you shampoo outdoors: Puppies generally do not appreciate cold water from a garden hose.) Either way, stick with the IGR type of insecticide. But *read labels* and only use if the label says the product is safe for young puppies. If you aren't sure, check with your veterinarian.

Make it a habit to brush the dog outside when you return from anywhere he might have picked up fleas or ticks. Spray at regular intervals suggested by the manufacturer.

Wash and treat all the dog's bedding. Stay with one brand of products that are made to be used together. Mixing and matching these chemical ingredients could be dangerous. Dispose of the containers as suggested on the can or bottle.

TREATING THE YARD

Outdoors, keep the grass short and use a spray made specifically for the yard and garden. These are potent insecticides. Treat them with respect and follow directions to the letter.

Ticks

Ticks are rapidly catching up with fleas in many areas of the country as the most invasive insect, especially the tiny deer ticks (found on whitetail deer and white-footed mice) that are the carriers of Lyme disease, which infects dogs and humans.

LYME DISEASE

The first sign of Lyme disease is a round red "target," which is easily seen on a person, but not on a furry dog! The next symptoms are fever, lethargy, and a swollen joint with intense arthritic-like pain. Check with your veterinarian if any of these things are apparent, especially if they occur after you have removed a tick. Antibiotics are successful in treating Lyme.

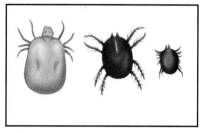

Three types of ticks (l-r): the wood tick, brown dog tick and deer tick.

Dogs can now be vaccinated annually against Lyme disease. Ask your veterinarian if it's appropriate for your dog, and at what age your dog should begin receiving it.

The most common variety of tick is the brown dog tick. They are about the size of a match head, but grow to that of a pebble when engorged with blood. Deer ticks are about the size of a sesame seed even when engorged—extremely difficult to find. Look for ticks behind the ears (or on them), on the neck and tummy, behind the elbows, between the toes and on the flanks.

TO REMOVE A TICK

Saturate a cotton ball with alcohol, nailpolish remover (acetone) or even gin. Dab the tick with the soaked cotton ball. This will stun it, causing it to lose its grip. Wait a few seconds, then use tweezers held close to the skin; with a steady, firm pull draw the tick out. The blood of an engorged tick is as dangerous to you as to your dog, so try not to crush the tick.

If you're squeamish, there's a small plastic device called a Tick-Pick (in pet stores) that is easy to use. Dispose of the tick (or take it to your vet for testing if you think it's a deer tick and your dog has not been immunized). Clean the area with an antiseptic and wash your hands thoroughly. Most flea repellents also deter ticks.

Earmites

These are another kind of pesky external parasites. They are microscopic bugs that live in the ear canal, causing an infection or irritation common in puppies and young dogs. You'll suspect infection by the way the pup scratches its ears or violently shakes its head to relieve the intense itching.

Use tweezers to remove ticks from your dog.

Dogs' ears are extremely sensitive, so it's better not to go probing around in the ear canal beyond the normal gentle cleaning of the outer ear canal area (the part you can easily see). Don't try to treat ear mites yourself regardless of how many products you may find in the pet store. Let your veterinarian diagnose the problem, and show you exactly how to treat it. Ear mites are persistent little bugs and you'll have to keep up the treatment until they are well and truly gone.

Mange

There are two types of mange you need to be aware of in your puppy. **Demodectic mange** is caused by a mite and results in a loss of hair around the nose, mouth and eyelids in puppies. It tends to improve on its own, but don't ignore it! When it does get worse, with patches appearing almost anywhere on the dog, the treatment is long and not always successful. To put your mind at ease, check with your vet at the first sign of mange.

Sarcoptic mange (also called scabies) may be seen as a red rash (mite bites) with crusts or scabs. It is intensely itchy and appears mostly on ear tips and elbows. These mites are not too fussy about where they land, and you'll know they've picked on you if you are feeling itchy around your waistline. Don't panic. With normal cleanliness, it disappears in about three weeks. But do consult your veterinarian for a dip that will eliminate the problem on the dog in four to six weeks.

"Snow nose"

Snow nose has no known cause or cure, but it is only a cosmetic problem, not a matter of health. The condition refers to a normally colored nose that gradually loses pigmentation, usually in the winter, and regains it come summertime. Occasionally, as a dog matures, the "snow nose" becomes a permanent discoloration, anything from charcoal gray (or dusty rose in a normally liver nose) to white.

Problems of the Musculoskeletal System

Run your hands regularly over your dog to feel for any injuries.

You can prevent some harm to a puppy's bones and joints that is due to such things as excessive or inappropriate activity, an inadequate diet or accidental trauma. A playful puppy should not be encouraged to fly off a step like "Super Puppy," which can result in impaired bone growth, injured joints or strained muscles. Injury can also result indoors from a puppy sliding on a slippery, highly waxed floor. Some of this damage may be permanent, if only as the seat of arthritis in later years.

While there are serious reasons for a puppy to **limp,** the most frequent are apt to be a pulled muscle, minor injury to a toe or nail, or a foreign object caught in or between the pads of a foot. Check out those possibilities first. With crate rest and "necessary" trips outside kept brief and on leash, the puppy should show improvement in a day or two.

Dogs don't complain about pain or discomfort, and will summon every bit of physical and mental strength to keep up with you and meet your demands. This makes your evaluation of health situations difficult. If the dog exhibits pain in trying to get up or lie down, or when you touch the area, he needs to be looked at by your veterinarian.

Luxating patella occurs when the patella, or knee-cap, slides off course, causing the dog to limp but not necessarily to be in great pain. Pain does occur later when arthritis sets in. More often seen in small dogs of the toy breeds, patella luxation is corrected by surgery.

Herniated disc commonly occurs in Dachshunds and Pekingese with their short legs and long backs. Pick the dog up with great care, grasping him firmly around the rib cage and supporting the body length of the dog. Never pull the dog up by his front legs.

Your puppy's environment can affect his health—beware of slippery floors or high places. (Shiba Inu)

One more reason not to allow your puppy up on furniture: jumping off can cause a herniated disc or any one of numerous other injuries to bones and joints. A herniated disc is definitely a matter for veterinary care.

HIP DYSPLASIA

HD is a widespread congenital defect (but also influenced by environmental stress and nutritional imbalance) which occurs mainly, but not exclusively, in the larger, heavier breeds, causing lameness and pain in the hindquarters.

Here's a simple explanation of the disease: The "ball" at the tip of the thigh bone is normally held in the "socket" of the hip by tight ligaments. When those ligaments are loose, the "ball" is not held correctly in place, the socket erodes and the dog becomes painfully lame and is said to be dysplastic.

The Orthopedic Foundation for Animals (OFA) certifies the degree of canine hip dysplasia using X-rays of the hips taken when the dog is two years of age or older. These are read by radiologists, and the dog is graded to indicate the existence and extent of the dysplasia. For more information write OFA, University of Missouri, Columbia, MO 65211.

It's especially important with some breeds, like this Miniature Pinscher pup, to guard against rough or excessive play, since their limbs are more fragile.

A newer method of hip analysis, call PennHIP, accurately measures the laxity, or looseness, of the hips (0.0 is a "perfect" tight hip; the mean laxity for Golden Retrievers is 0.49) and can assess the susceptibility to HD in dogs as young as sixteen weeks. To locate a vet in your area who can do these PennHIP X-rays and evaluations, call 1-800-248-8099.

Hip dysplasia is a complex infirmity. Initial treatment is to minimize the pain, but many cases require surgery, even including hip replacement, with lifelong curtailment of exercise. Be alert to the warning signs—limping, rabbit-hopping, "yips" when lying down or getting up, cringing when you pat the hip area, difficulty (or refusal) to manage stairs. If your pup will weigh over thirty-five to forty pounds as an adult, you should be aware that he may become affected by HD.

Nutrition-related defects occur as much from too much (surplus vitamins, obesity from overfeeding) as well as from too little. "Environmental stress" refers to subjecting a growing puppy to excessive activities such as jogging, running or overly long walks, etc., all of which should be avoided until growth is complete.

Problems of the Respiratory System

The respiratory system of the dog has a different range of sounds from that of people. For example, there's sneezing that sounds like choking, coughing that sounds like a goose honking, sniffing or snuffling at everything. Differences are most noticeable in the *brachycephalic,* or short-nosed, dogs.

Puppies are prone to picking up kennel cough at places where a lot of other dogs congregate, such as a dog show. (Curly Coated Retrievers)

KENNEL COUGH

This is serious in puppies, but not in adult dogs. However, it is highly contagious and the dog must be kept isolated. It is characterized by a dry, harsh, hacking cough and occasionally a runny nose (especially in puppies), but otherwise the dog will seem to be healthy and bright.

Most cases are mild, lasting about two weeks. The dog needs a warm room and a vaporizer, preferably the cold-steam type. Take the dog's temperature daily. An elevated temperature indicates the presence of something more serious than kennel cough. For a persistent dry cough, a cough suppressant may be given, but check with your vet as to which product is suitable for your dog and the correct dosage. Keep in touch with your veterinarian, because bronchitis can develop from the original infection.

Kennel cough vaccine (given as a nasal spray) is a good precaution for every puppy going into kindergarten puppy training, for dogs in any training classes, or just with play-dates in the park, etc. It is a requirement of all well-run boarding kennels.

BRONCHITIS

Bronchitis is often a complication of another respiratory infection, such as kennel cough. The cough is similar, sometimes followed by retching. The dog acts and looks sick and may or may not have a temperature. Your veterinarian will prescribe antibiotics, bed rest and also moderate exercise to aid bronchial drainage.

PNEUMONIA

Pneumonia is an infection of the lungs that can result from the kennel cough virus, but in puppies is primarily the bacterial type. There are several other types of pneumonia, but all are characterized by a high temperature, coughing, rapid breathing and pulse, and the telltale "rattling" sounds in the chest. This is *serious.* Get to the vet!

RUNNY NOSE

Runny nose is a symptom of many illnesses. The dog should be examined by the veterinarian before it gets worse.

Problems of the Heart

Most congenital heart defects that occur in people also occur in dogs. Your veterinarian will pick up any abnormality on your first and subsequent visits. It is not unusual to hear a "heart murmur" (caused by a mal-formation at birth) in a very young puppy, only to have the problem resolve itself to become almost normal in the adult. But since congenital defects can also prove fatal, especially when several are present, the vet will want to monitor the situation closely.

Problems of the Eyes, Ears and Mouth

EYES

Any change in the appearance of the eyes—watering, dryness, itching, redness, discharge, color—calls for a prompt visit to the vet. Sight is very precious and minor problems that can be easily corrected can just as easily worsen if left untreated.

Squeeze eye ointment into the lower lid.

Cataracts (opaque spots on the lens of the eye) affect the vision and can occur at any age, but most commonly in dogs under the age of five. Certain breeds are predisposed to inherited cataracts. In very young dogs, the condition is some-times referred to as juvenile cataract. As with people, cataracts are also part of the aging process. Cataracts also occur in diabetic dogs. You can't tell by looking at the dog's eyes how much vision is retained, but the presence of a cataract does not mean the dog is, or even will be, blind. There is no treatment, but in certain cases surgery may be possible.

Conjunctivitis is an inflammation of the inner mem-brane of the eye, which becomes red, with a discharge that is watery if the cause is a foreign object (dirt, hair), or thick and pus-like if bacterial or viral. A veterinar-ian's diagnosis is needed before treatment is started.

Entropion and **ectropion** are conditions of the eyelid. *Entropion* indicates an eyelid (usually the lower lid) is turned in, causing the eyelashes to irritate the cornea. It is most often genetic, but can be caused by an eye

124

injury. *Ectropion* is the reverse, and the eyelid turns out. This is most often seen in breeds with sagging facial skin, or in older dogs with a loss of skin tone. The danger to the eye is exposure. The only treatment in either case is surgery.

Progressive retinal atrophy (PRA) is a genetic disease that is unfortunately common in many breeds. The cells of the retina gradually deteriorate, causing blindness. The saddest part of PRA is that it can occur at any age from puppyhood on and there is no known cure.

Watery eye is a problem in many small breeds, often brought on by inadequate drainage of the natural eye fluids. It causes discoloration of surrounding hair and can even be the source of skin infection. Flushing the tear ducts may correct the situation; otherwise surgery is indicated. Keeping the area around the eye free of hair, careful cleansing of the eye and the skin, and adequate protection against shampoo getting into the eyes are all part of the constant care of a dog with this problem.

Breeds with sagging facial skin, like this Mastiff puppy, are more prone to ectropion.

Dry eye occurs when the production of tears is inadequate to keep the cornea lubricated. Treatment involves putting "artificial tears" (drops) in the eyes several times a day. Some cases can be helped by surgery.

EARS

A dog's hearing is far more sensitive than a human's, with an added range of high-frequency sounds. That's why we rely on the dog to be our first alert. Dogs' ears must be kept clean and free of mites, dirt, excessive wax and hair. Wipe each ear with a separate cotton ball that has been slightly dampened in warm water. Use a cotton swab to clean the sides of the outer ear canal, but be wary of pushing debris down into the canal. If you aren't sure, ask your vet or groomer to show you how. Healthy ears smell clean.

Deafness is a congenital defect in certain breeds, and breeders are working with researchers to eliminate the problem. As in people, there are degrees of deafness, but even a totally deaf young dog can lead a full, happy life. A loss of hearing is normal in the aging dog.

Infections in the ear, when caught in time, are easily treated. That's why it is important to wipe out the ear and sniff for any offensive odor every week during routine grooming. If neglected, an infection can be extremely painful for the dog. Symptoms include odor, excessive wax, head-shaking, rubbing the head on the ground, pawing with front feet and/or scratching with hind feet. Sometimes this scratching to relieve the pain is enough to cause an open wound in the cheek area. Do not try to treat an ear infection yourself. Because of its "L" shape, you could damage the ear canal.

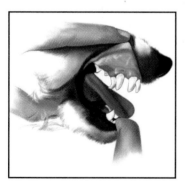

Mites are the common cause of most ear problems. They are discussed on page 118.

MOUTH

In order to avoid infection, it is essential to keep any **folds of skin** around the mouth clean and free of food—easily taken care of when brushing the dog's teeth. (See page 127.)

Check your dog's teeth frequently and brush them regularly.

Foreign objects in the mouth must be removed immediately. However, it isn't always easy to do. For example, it's not unusual for a stick or rawhide the pup is chewing on to become lodged in the roof of the mouth. Even with a small puppy, it often takes two people—one to hold the frantically squirming pup, the other to remove the obstruction. A dab of peanut butter on the dog's tongue sometimes helps, too (as a distraction).

Care must always be taken not to push a foreign object down the throat. Hook your finger *behind* the object so that you are pulling it forward. But that, of course, means you are pulling from a broader area into a narrower one. As you can see, this can quickly turn into an emergency. If the object goes down the throat, or you can't dislodge it, get to your veterinarian immediately. This may be the time you'll have to use an emergency animal hospital.

When the obstruction is already lodged in the throat, the signs of distress will include slobbering, inability to swallow (even water) without pain or discomfort, accompanied by what may appear to be attempts to "cough up" the object. Take immediate action.

With a puppy, investigate anything suspicious. An innocent piece of thread hanging from his mouth can have a needle at the other end stuck in the tongue or gums.

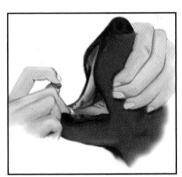

To give a pill, open the mouth wide, then drop it in the back of the throat.

Puppy teeth fall out and a permanent set comes in, only sometimes the little ones don't fall out. It's not unusual (in some breeds it is very common) to retain puppy teeth, but they need to be removed by your veterinarian before they cause malocclusion. Depending on which teeth are involved, it could require an anesthetic, which poses a problem for the short-nosed breeds. Some puppy teeth come out readily.

Brushing your dog's teeth is another "must." Do it as part of the grooming routine, plus two or three times more during the week. The easiest way is to use a canine toothbrush and toothpaste. (Do *not* use people toothpaste since a dog doesn't spit it out and it can cause stomach upsets.) A small puppy has no problem letting you put your finger in its mouth, and this method can be continued, using a gauze

127

pad wrapped around your finger and dipped in (dog) toothpaste or a baking soda and water paste. Lift the lip gently and rub the outsides and gumline of all the teeth. Some dogs enjoy having their mouth sprayed with plain water when the tooth-brushing is over.

Your dog will still need to have his teeth examined at least once a year by the veterinarian to keep the teeth, gums and mouth healthy. If routine care is overlooked, gingivitis and periodontitis (and bad breath) will be next—just like in people!

Tonsillitis is a disease mainly of puppies or young dogs and seen mostly in small breeds. However, the dog typically runs a high fever and shows all the usual signs of being sick. The treatment is much the same as for people—liquids and antibiotics. Check with your veterinarian for diagnosis and prescription.

Problems of the Gastrointestinal System

Intestinal upsets, whether an actual disease or infection, or from having eaten forbidden food, are all too common in puppies. Everything that is in reach goes into the mouth and ends up in the stomach! If you know when unauthorized food went down, you'll know to watch for constipation or diarrhea.

More serious is the **swallowed object** that is not food, but a toy, plastic, metal, cloth, etc., because such things can lodge in the intestinal tract and require surgery to remove. Puppies (of all ages) have been known to swallow pantyhose, socks, T-shirts, coins, nails . . . you name it and some veterinarian will have removed it! If caught immediately, something like a soft latex toy can be brought up by induced vomiting.

Gastrointestinal upsets are among the easiest health problems to recognize because the symptoms are diarrhea or constipation, excessive drinking and urinating, and/or vomiting. In some cases the puppy will otherwise appear to be healthy, but usually the dog's body language is "down": ears held back and down, tail down, head down.

Constipation may be caused by any indigestible thing a dog eats or by a lack of fiber in the diet. A dog normally defecates two to four times a day, so if an entire day goes by without the dog passing stool (or passing watery or bloody stool), he is constipated. Your veterinarian will want to see the dog if the problem doesn't clear up in twenty-four to forty-eight hours.

Because puppies chew and eat almost anything, they tend to get upset stomachs. Keep anything your puppy may choke or get sick on out of his reach! (German Shepherd Dog)

Diarrhea is a common symptom of many things, ranging from a minor digestive upset to extremely serious disease. At the onset of diarrhea or very loose stools, withhold food (but not water) for a day, but contact your veterinarian immediately. He may suggest a "people remedy"—Kaopectate or Pepto-Bismol—but don't give it without a vet's instructions since the dosage depends on the size and age of your dog.

Other, more serious diseases of which diarrhea is a symptom include such things as *Coccidia*, *Giardia* and worms, all intestinal parasites and treatable given prompt attention.

Vomiting is something dogs seem to do easily and often without a verifiable reason. For example, dogs often vomit after eating grass—to a point where it is thought they may eat grass *in order to vomit*! If your dog vomits more than a couple of times, or heaves without ejecting anything more than clear or yellow liquid, get on the phone to the vet. If the vomiting is in conjunction with any other symptom, such as diarrhea or pain, it is a serious condition and must be seen by the veterinarian.

Bloat, also known as acute gastric dilatation-torsion, occurs speedily and can be fatal. Primarily seen in large, deep-chested adult dogs, the stomach fills up with gas or fluid and as it swells, twists around. The dog goes into shock and immediate surgery is the only way to save the dog at that point. Bloat most often occurs a couple of hours after the dog has eaten a large meal and had a quantity of water, followed by exercise. The dog appears restless, the stomach swells and becomes hard. Time is the most important factor—get to a vet *immediately*. Dogs that may be candidates for bloat should be fed several small meals and offered water only between meals, not immediately after. Bloat is something to discuss with your veterinarian until all your questions have been answered.

Eating stool (Coprophagy) This is really a people problem, because it is not a problem to the dog. The only harm to come of it is if the ingested stool contains parasites (or their eggs). Puppies and bitches are more apt to eat their stool than are adult males, which may be attributed to the fact that the mother cleans her puppies from the day they are born as nature's way of keeping the den clean. People, quite naturally, find it disgusting (as well as almost impossible to pronounce!).

One way to stop a dog from doing this is to put meat tenderizer in the dog's food; another way is to add K-Zyme (a pet product containing natural minerals) to the food. Of course, the best way is to take your dog, on leash, and stand until he has defecated. You'll be right there to indicate your displeasure—*accht!*—as the dog turns to sniff. On walks, use the command, "Leave it!"

Problems of the Neurological System

Distemper is the primary killer of puppies worldwide because it is highly contagious (three to fifteen days from exposure to onset) and takes many different forms. The first symptoms are often those of a common cold (which of course dogs do not get) with a high fever. The discharge from the nose and eyes turns from thin and clear to thick and yellow. The disease progresses to the brain, and in most cases the dog dies from that involvement or the complications that follow. There is no cure, but there *is* vaccine. The "D" in DHLPP (which every puppy should have) stands for Distemper.

Epilepsy is a congenital or acquired disorder typically seen as recurring seizures. There are numerous variations—*petit mal* (mild seizures of short duration) and

grand mal, in which the seizures are prolonged with total body involvement. It is frightening to witness a seizure, but important that you do not try in any way to handle a dog during one. Most last up to five minutes, with a secondary phase where the dog is still disoriented and wobbly, which can last any time up to two hours. It's essential that you remain calm and quiet until the dog is completely back to normal. Contact your vet at once if your dog has a

seizure. There is no cure for epilepsy, but there are means of controlling the extent of the seizures.

Puppies that spend a lot of time outside may encounter rabid wildlife. Be sure your pup is vaccinated against rabies, and if you see wildlife acting strangely, tell an animal control officer. (Brittany)

Rabies is a fatal disease that cannot be diagnosed except through an autopsy. In most of the U.S., vaccination programs are in place and are effectively controlling the disease in our pet animals. There are occasional outbursts of rabies among skunks, raccoons, foxes and bats, so no one should ever touch any wild animal that seems friendly or tries to approach people. That is not normal behavior. Alert an animal control officer if you see a wild animal acting this way.

Rabies vaccine that gives one-year protection can be given to puppies, and to adult dogs in a form that lasts three years. Many local ordinances require proof of rabies vaccination at the time of licensing.

Problems of the Urinary System

A urinary tract disorder should be suspected if your housetrained dog loses control and begins to wet anywhere and everywhere in the house, or tries to void but appears to be in pain, or drinks the water bowl dry no matter how often you fill it. Any such abnormality is reason enough for you to contact the veterinarian. The quicker diagnosis is made and treatment begun, the less chance there is for the condition to become more serious (kidney failure, for example) and therefore more difficult to treat.

Prostatitis occurs in unneutered males and is indicated by fever and painful urination (even dripping pus), with the dog standing hunched up and in obvious discomfort. This infection is successfully treated with antibiotics. Once prostatitis is eliminated, having the dog neutered prevents a repeat infection. Have your dog neutered first and you won't have to worry about prostatitis.

Male/Female Problems

THE DOG (MALE)

A normal male dog has two **testicles** descended into the scrotum by the age of six months. Prior to that, one or both testicles may go back up into the groin temporarily when the puppy is cold, playing or otherwise excited. After six months, if only one testicle has descended into the scrotum, the dog is called monorchid; if neither testicle is down, the dog is cryptorchid. The condition is of concern to breeders because it is an inherited defect. If this happens to your pet, check with your vet regarding neutering, but it is helpful also to inform the breeder, who will use the information in planning future breedings. For information on neutering, see page 113.

The mature male normally has a small amount of white or yellowish discharge from the skin covering the penis, which the dog cleans. Excessive, darker discharge with a foul odor is indicative of infection. Your veterinarian will show you how to treat it.

THE FEMALE (BITCH)

Mammary gland tumors—half of which are malignant in female dogs—are virtually eliminated by having the bitch spayed prior to the onset of sexual maturity (or the first estrus), which normally occurs at about six months of age. The same is true of cancer of the uterus.

Pyometra is another very serious disease in which the uterus fills with pus. It is fatal if not promptly treated. But it is entirely preventable: Have your bitch spayed.

Vaginitis can be detected by excessive licking of the vulva in the bitch's effort to clean herself. The hair around the vulva may be stained. Another sign is painful urination. The infection is treated with antibiotics and douches.

Spaying   See page 113.

First Aid and Emergencies

Your puppy cannot tell you when he is sick, but if you spend enough time with him and are observant of his behavior, you'll notice when he's feeling off. The following are examples of problems that require first aid.

First aid is what you do to assist a dog in an emergency situation before you reach the vet's office. Such assistance should be minimal, so as

---

A FIRST-AID KIT

Keep a canine first-aid kit on hand for general care and emergencies. Check it periodically to make sure liquids haven't spilled or dried up, and replace medications and materials after they're used. Your kit should include:

Activated charcoal tablets

Adhesive tape
(1 and 2 inches wide)

Antibacterial ointment
(for skin and eyes)

Aspirin (buffered or enteric coated, *not* Ibuprofen)

Bandages: Gauze rolls (1 and 2 inches wide) and dressing pads

Cotton balls

Diarrhea medicine

Dosing syringe

Hydrogen peroxide (3%)

Petroleum jelly

Rectal thermometer

Rubber gloves

Rubbing alcohol

Scissors

Tourniquet

Towel

Tweezers

133

not to make matters worse, and it must be safe for the dog and its rescuer. If possible, alert the veterinarian immediately.

The first rule of canine first aid is for the rescuer to remain completely calm and (outwardly at least) in control of the situation. The second rule is to fight off the desire to pick up or lean over to comfort a hurt dog face-to-face the way you would a child. When hurt and frightened, a dog's instinct for self-preservation takes over; it is likely to bite whatever comes near. That's where safety comes in.

An Elizabethan collar keeps your dog from licking a fresh wound.

In an Emergency

If something happens to your puppy during non-regular veterinary visiting hours, it's important to have an emergency number to call. Ask your veterinarian for this number on your first visit and keep it by the phone. You won't want to be scrambling for it when a real emergency strikes. And you won't want to be struggling with directions in the middle of the night if you've never been to the emergency clinic before. It's a good idea to do a practice run to the emergency clinic during a non-emergency. You'll need all the calm you can muster in a real emergency, and knowing how long it will take to get to the clinic is important.

Typical First-Aid Situations

When you notice anything unusual in the way your puppy is acting, ask yourself these questions:

What caused you to think there was a problem?

What was your first clue there was something wrong?

Is your puppy eating normally?

Does your puppy have a temperature? (Instructions on how to take your puppy's temperature are on page 107.)

What do his stools look like?

Is your puppy limping?

When you do a hands-on exam, is he sore anywhere? Can you feel a lump? Is anything red or swollen?

Write down anything you've noticed. When you call your veterinarian, be prepared to give specific details.

Restraints   Having established the fact that hurting dogs bite, before attempting to muzzle him, be certain he is breathing normally since limited breathing could be made worse by keeping the dog's mouth closed. Don't have a muzzle handy? No problem. A necktie, pantyhose, two feet of rope or a dog leash will do nicely. Tie a loose knot in the middle and slip the loop of the knot over the middle of the dog's nose. Pull it firm and tie the two ends under the dog's chin, then in back of the dog's ears. (Make that last tie a bow so it will untie easily to pull forward and off the nose.)

Use a scarf or old hose to make a temporary muzzle, as shown.

Dogs with short noses or no discernible bridge, such as Pugs, Pekingese and Bulldogs, are not candidates for a makeshift muzzle. In fact, don't do anything that might interfere with their breathing. If you have assistance, a rolled-up blanket, towel or a pillow can be held (gently, but firmly) around the dog's neck while treating the injury.

Shock Many things such as dehydration or poisoning cause a dog to go into shock, but being hit by a car is the major cause of shock. Since "shock" refers to the breakdown of the cardiovascular system, immediate veterinary care is essential.

Electrical shock is the fate of a puppy left to chew on an electric cord his owner forgot to put up out of reach. The result is a nasty burn to the mouth which, while painful, will heal in time. More serious are lightning strikes or touching downed wires, as in either case the dog (if not killed) is burned and also suffers circulatory (heart) collapse and pulmonary (lung) edema. If the dog is unconscious and not breathing, give artificial respiration. No matter what the condition, get to a veterinarian immediately.

Hit by car Automobiles still account for most canine deaths, which is a sad commentary on our responsible dog ownership. All it takes to keep your dog safe is a leash or a fence and basic obedience training. No matter how slight the injury may seem, any dog hit by a car requires immediate emergency treatment by a veterinarian. There may be internal injuries or bleeding, broken bones, concussion and so forth. (See "Shock," above.)

Check for external bleeding and stop it by applying a pressure bandage or just holding a bandage or clean padded cloth over the wound. Spurting blood indicates a severed artery, which can also be controlled by applying pressure on the artery.

Moving an injured dog other than a very small one requires two people and a board (bench, sled or any improvised stretcher) or a blanket held taut. Do not muzzle a dog in shock, but keep the dog quiet and transfer him immediately to the veterinarian's.

When a board is the means of transportation, be sure the dog is securely tied to it with strips of sheeting or rope. An injured animal panics easily and could do itself further damage in struggling to escape.

Life-Saving Procedures

There are three things you should know how to do that could instantly save your dog's life. Artificial respiration, to start the dog breathing again, and heart massage, used when no heartbeat can be felt or heard, together form the well-known **CPR** (for cardio-pulmonary resuscitation). The **Heimlich maneuver** is the method used to dislodge a foreign object that is causing the dog to choke.

CHEST COMPRESSION

The easiest way to administer artificial respiration is by compressing the chest. Here is the five-step method for chest compression:

1. Feel or listen for a pulse or heartbeat.

2. Clear the mouth of secretions and foreign objects. (You might have to use the Heimlich maneuver to remove an obstruction that's out of reach.)

3. Lay the dog on his *right* side on a flat surface.

4. Place both hands on the chest and press down sharply, releasing immediately.

(If you do *not* hear air going in and out, switch to the mouth-to-nose method.)

5. Continue until the dog is breathing on his own, or as long as the heart is beating.

Mouth-to-Nose Method Follow steps 1 and 2 above, then

3. Pull the tongue forward and keep the lips closed with your hand.

4. Take a breath and, with your mouth over the dog's nose, blow a steady stream of air for three seconds.

5. Release to let the air out. Continue until the dog is breathing or as long as the heart is beating.

HEART MASSAGE

When heart massage is combined with mouth-to-nose resuscitation (it takes two people), it is canine CPR. Heart massage alone, however, also brings air to the lungs.

To perform, follow steps 1 and 2 above for artificial respiration, then for *small dogs and puppies:*

3. Standing in back of the dog, place one hand on the sternum (bottom of chest) behind the dog's elbow with your thumb on top, fingers beneath.

4. With the other hand above your thumb, over the heart, press the chest firmly six times. Count to five (to let the chest expand) and repeat until the heart is beating or no heartbeat is felt for five minutes.

For *large dogs,* follow the same procedure but place the heel of your hand on the rib cage behind the elbow (which will be over the heart).

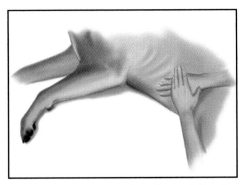

Applying abdominal thrusts can save a choking dog.

THE HEIMLICH MANEUVER

This is the method used to clear the dog's air passage when he's choking. He'll be breathing hard, coughing, pawing at his mouth and in a panic. Put one hand over his nose, pressing down on his lips with your thumb and forefinger. With your other hand, press down the lower jaw to pry his mouth open.

If you can't see anything or feel anything with a finger, lay the dog on his side and lower his head by putting a pillow under his hindquarters. On a puppy or small dog, place one hand a couple of inches below the bottom of his ribcage (the sternum) and the other hand on the dog's back for support. (On a larger dog, place both hands below the sternum.) Press *sharply* in and up. Keep it up until the foreign object is dislodged. What you are doing is literally "knocking the air out of him" so the object is expelled by the force of the air. Should the dog be unconscious, do artificial respiration and get on your way to the veterinarian.

Burns are caused by many things, such as touching a hot surface, fire and even sunburn. Severe burn of any kind can proceed to shock and the prognosis is poor. Small superficial burns can be treated by soaking with cold water or ice packs for fifteen to twenty minutes just to relieve the pain. Then trim surrounding hair, wash with surgical soap and gently blot dry. Apply antibiotic ointment. If the area needs protection (for example, when the dog lies down or walks), wrap it loosely with gauze.

Bleeding is one of the primary concerns for first aid. Bleeding of a minor wound can be stopped by first cleaning the area with antiseptic and applying a gauze pad, then bandaging with even pressure using gauze or any clean available material. Watch for signs of swelling or discoloration below the bandage which indicates a loss of circulation, in which case loosen or remove the bandage immediately.

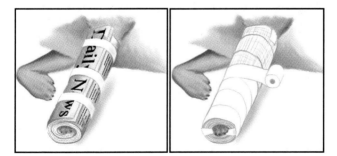

Make a temporary splint by wrapping the leg in firm casing, then bandaging it.

Arterial bleeding comes in bright red spurts and requires a thick pressure pad (as above) plus additional pressure applied by hand. A tourniquet can be applied to the tail or leg above the wound, between the wound and the heart, but it *must* be loosened every twenty-five to thirty minutes and is best left to a professional.

Broken bones may be made worse by handling. In puppies the most common break is a "greenstick fracture." A compound fracture (where the skin is pierced by the broken bone) should first be covered with a clean cloth. Immobilize the area and transport the dog (preferably on a rigid surface) as carefully and quickly as possible to a veterinarian.

Convulsions and seizures Remain calm and move out of the way anything the dog might bump into. The dog will not swallow his tongue—that's a myth. Time the seizure and observe the extent of body involvement so you can inform the veterinarian when you call. Keep the dog calm and quiet after he returns to normal.

Cuts and abrasions should be washed with warm soap and water, then rinsed with cold water to help stop bleeding. Apply an antiseptic spray or ointment.

Dog fights are very dangerous for dogs and people. If two dogs cannot be pulled apart by means of their leashes, separating them is best left to a pair of strong men, who will probably be bitten in the process no matter what means of separation they try. A harsh stream of cold water may work sometimes, but not often enough to recommend it. Throwing a coat or blanket over the two heads will often cause one of the dogs to let go for an instant—but in that instant, someone has to be ready to pull them apart by their tails or hindquarters.

IDENTIFYING YOUR DOG

It's a terrible thing to think about, but your dog could somehow, someday, get lost or stolen. How would you get him back? Your best bet would be to have some form of identification on your dog. You can choose from a collar and tags, a tattoo, a microchip or a combination of these three.

Every dog should wear a buckle collar with identification tags. They are the quickest and easiest way for a stranger to identify your dog. It's best to inscribe the tags with your name and phone number; you don't need to include your dog's name.

There are two ways to permanently identify your dog. The first is a tattoo, placed on the inside of your dog's thigh. The tattoo should be your social security number or your dog's AKC registration number.

The second is a microchip, a rice-sized pellet that's inserted under the dog's skin at the base of the neck, between the shoulder blades. When a scanner is passed over the dog, it will beep, notifying the person that the dog has a chip. The scanner will then show a code, identifying the dog. Microchips are becoming more and more popular and are certainly the wave of the future.

A shrill personal alarm (used to deter a hold-up) may work. Mace or mace-type spray may work. Avoid inflicting pain on either dog because it will only increase the dog's aggression. Avoid giving the appearance of siding with either dog. Clean all bite wounds thoroughly, especially small puncture wounds, and get the dog(s) to the veterinarian at once.

Drowning Dogs do not know how to swim naturally, and too often they get into the water, manage to swim a short distance and then are unable to get out. This is especially true in pools. Treatment is the same as for people. Get the dog onto land immediately, clean out his mouth, give mouth-to-nose resuscitation or even oxygen if available. Be prepared to treat for shock.

Hypothermia occurs when a dog is exposed to extreme cold. For some dogs, just getting wet and moderately cold will cause the body temperature to drop dangerously. Bring the dog into a warm room. Wrap him in blankets, rub him with towels and place hot water bottles (containing *warm* water) under armpits, chest and stomach. When rectal temperature reaches 100 degrees, feed honey or sugar and water.

Heat Stroke requires immediate action. Most dogs suffering from heatstroke were left in cars. Even with the windows partially open and parked in the shade, on a moderately warm day it only takes minutes for the inside of a car to become a deathtrap. Dogs do not sweat, but pant to breathe in cool air. When the air becomes as warm as the dog's body temperature, this body-cooling system fails and the dog can suffer brain damage, go into a coma and die in rapid succession.

Speedy treatment is essential. Remove the dog to a cool place. Immerse him in a tub of water if possible, or wet him down with a garden hose or buckets of water. Wrap the dog in wet towels; add ice packs to the head, neck and groin area if possible *and get to a veterinarian immediately.*

Poisons Because puppies are so curious, they are prone to getting into any number of potentially toxic substances. These include houseplants, outdoor plants, household substances like cleaning products, pesticides and medications, and other chemical-based products like paint thinner, kerosene and so on.

Specific plants were discussed in some detail in Chapter 3, pages 19 to 21. One of the most deadly substances is antifreeze, which tastes sweet to dogs. A few licks result in kidney damage. Only slightly more than that ends in death. Get veterinary help at once. There is no home treatment.

Some of the many household substances harmful to your dog.

About Aspirin Aspirin is not toxic to dogs at doses recommended by a veterinarian, though it has been known to cause stomach irritation. It's best to give a dog a buffered or enteric-coated aspirin. *Tylenol, ibuprofen and naproxen sodium are all toxic to dogs.*

Porcupine quills are painful and usually hit the face, which makes them difficult and painful to remove. Since the dog will have to be sedated or anesthetized, removal calls for veterinary skill. If there are just one or two and you want to do it yourself, use pliers (preferably the needlenose type) placed close to the skin and draw the quill out in the same direction it went in. If one should break, it's off to the vet's for surgical removal.

Some **topical irritants** that dogs get into include such things as tar or grease and can be safely removed by working vegetable or mineral oil into the coat and washing with a mild detergent. There's only one solution for getting rid of oil-based paint on a dog's coat—cut away the hair. *Never* use turpentine, kerosene or gasoline to remove these substances. Just inhaling these harsh products causes pneumonia, which in turn is life-threatening. (Signs of such inhalation include vomiting, tremors, convulsions and coma.)

Skunked! The bane of every country or suburban dog's owner is the small black and white skunk. A large can of plain tomato juice is an old standby—and it works, but don't try it on a dog with a long white coat. A large dog will require several cans.

There are several new products on the market to eliminate skunk odor. You'll need to toss out the sprayed collar and leash (remove ID or rabies tags first) because the smell will never go away. Shampoo and rinse the dog several times (preferably outdoors), following product directions. Some groomers and some veterinary hospitals offer this service. If you find one in your area that does, add them to your emergency phone numbers list!

Snakes and Other Critters

Snakes and toads fascinate puppies by their slithery or erratic movement, but some varieties are dangerous playmates. Most snakes (even the ones that bite) are non-poisonous and no cause for alarm; still, it pays to check on what your pup is playing with in the garden.

There are only four poisonous varieties in the U.S.— **cottonmouths** (a.k.a. water moccasins), **copperheads, rattlesnakes** and **coral snakes.** One way to tell the difference (but only after the attack) is by the presence of fang marks, which are only in the bite of poisonous snakes, although this identification is lost on a densely coated dog.

Your library is a good source of information (including color illustrations) of snakes because it is seldom appropriate to get close enough to the head and mouth to see which type is confronting you or your dog!

The reaction to a bite is immediate and the symptoms are similar to those of other kinds of poisoning— panting, drooling, restlessness, weakness and finally shock and even death. The bite of a coral snake results in excruciating pain, vomiting, diarrhea, convulsions and coma. That is the worst-case scenario. The site of the attack (when you can locate it) shows rapid reaction, with swelling, redness and extreme pain in the area.

Because of the intense pain, the first thing to do is restrain the dog and get to the veterinarian immediately. Familiarize yourself with the snake-bite kit in your first aid kit (it's in there!) because you will have to take over if it will take time to reach the vet.

If it's possible to kill the snake, take the remains with you for positive identification.

Toads taste awful, so there will be frothing at the mouth and drooling, but only one species of toad (Bufo) is poisonous. It is found in southern states. Death from a Bufo bite can occur in as little as fifteen minutes. Flush the dog's mouth, using a hose if possible, and induce vomiting by giving one to three teaspoons of hydrogen peroxide (three percent) every ten minutes, or place one-half to one teaspoon of salt at the back of the tongue. *Get to a vet!*

Giving Your Puppy Medicine

Some medicines are easy to administer, some are not. Some puppies will take pills or let you put ointment in their eyes easily, some will not. Ask your veterinarian for help and follow these instructions.

To put **eye ointment** in the eye without poking the puppy with the tube, stand behind your puppy and cuddle his head up against your legs. With one hand, gently pull the lower eyelid away from the eye just slightly. At the same time, squeeze some of the ointment into the lower eyelid. When the puppy closes its eye, the medication will be distributed over the eye.

There are a couple of different ways to **give your puppy a pill**. The easiest way is to keep a jar of baby food on hand. Dip the pill in it and your pup should readily lick the pill (with baby food) right from your hand. For those who lick up the food and spit out the pill, you'll need to be more careful. Have your puppy sit and stand behind him, straddling his back. With the pill in one hand, pull your puppy's head up and back gently so his muzzle is pointing up. Open his mouth and very quickly drop the pill in the back of his throat. Close his mouth and massage his throat until he swallows. Before you let him go, open his mouth and check to see that the pill is gone. Follow up with a treat.

You can give **liquid medication** the same way, pouring it into your puppy's mouth. Be careful that he doesn't inhale the medication instead of swallow it. An easier way is to measure the medicine into a chicken or turkey baster or a large eyedropper, put the tip of the baster into the puppy's mouth from the side (between the molars) and, holding the puppy's mouth shut, squeeze the medication in while you tilt his head backwards slightly so the medicine runs into instead of out of the mouth.

Applying **skin ointments** is usually very easy—just part the hair so you're putting the ointment directly on the skin and rub it in according to directions. Keeping your puppy from licking the ointment off can be more difficult, and licking often makes matters worse. If your puppy has a bad skin condition or stitches that need to heal, your veterinarian will probably give you an Elizabethan collar for him. Named for the fashion styles of the reign of Queen Elizabeth I, this is a large plastic collar that extends at least to the tip of your puppy's nose. The collar is ugly and clumsy, and most puppies absolutely hate it, but it's the only way the wound will have a chance to heal.

Remember, whenever your veterinarian prescribes a treatment or medication, don't be afraid to ask questions. Ask what the drug(s) is, what it does and how long your puppy should take it. Ask if there are any side effects you should watch for. Make sure you understand what your puppy's problem is, what the course of treatment will do and what you should (or should not) expect. That done, make sure you follow through on the course of treatment. If your veterinarian said to give the medication for ten days, give it for ten days. Don't stop at five days just because your puppy looks better. Again, if you have any problems or reservations, call your vet.

Poison Control

The National Animal Poison Control Center (NAPCC) provides service twenty-four hours a day, with forty-four licensed veterinarians and board-certified toxicologists to aid you. When you call **1-800-548-2423** you will be charged thirty dollars per case (only payable by credit card) and there's no charge for follow-up calls. Calling **1-900-680-0000** will give you five minutes for twenty dollars plus $2.95 for each additional minute (no follow-ups). Put both numbers with your emergency telephone numbers. Put copies in the glove compartment of your car and in your first aid kit. Be prepared to give your name, address and phone number, what your puppy got into—the amount and how long ago—your pup's breed, age, sex and weight and what reaction the pup is experiencing.

As Your Puppy Ages

It may not seem like he'll ever grow up when he's in the prime of puppyhood, but he will. In fact, dogs can, on the average, live up to 14 years. To live that long in good health, however, your puppy will need your help.

As your puppy ages, you'll notice certain changes. The intense teething period will subside, upward growth will slow down and your puppy will start to "fill out," he'll need less food, his energy level will decrease slightly, and you may even notice greying around his muzzle.

Depending on the kind of dog you have, as he hits middle to old age, your dog's vision will dim, his hearing fade and his joints stiffen. Heart and kidney disease are common in older dogs. Reflexes will not be as sharp as they once were, and your dog may be more sensitive to heat and cold. Your dog may also get grouchy, showing less tolerance to younger dogs, children and other things that may not be part of his normal routine.

Arthritis Arthritis is common in old dogs. The joints get stiff, especially when it's chilly. Your dog may have trouble getting up in the morning. Make sure he has something soft and warm to sleep on not just at night, but all day. Talk to your veterinarian about treatment; there are pain relievers that can help.

Nutrition   As your dog's activity level slows down, he will need to consume less calories and, as his body ages, he will need less protein. However, some old dogs have a problem digesting foods, too, and this may show up in poor stools and a dull coat. Several dog food manufacturers offer premium quality foods for senior dogs; these foods are more easily digested by the old dog.

Exercise   Exercise is still important to your old dog, who needs the stimulation of walking around and seeing and smelling the world. A leisurely walk around the neighborhood might be enough.

When It's Time   There will come a time when you know your dog is suffering more than he needs to, and you will have to decide how to put him out of his pain. Only you can make the decision, but spare your companion the humiliation of incontinence, convulsions or the inability to stand up or move around. Your veterinarian can advise you on the condition of your dog, but don't let him or her make this decision for you.

When you know it's time, call your veterinarian. He or she can give your dog a tranquilizer, then an injection that is an overdose of anesthetic. Your already sleepy dog will quietly stop breathing. Be there with your dog. Let your arms hold your old friend and let your dog hear your voice saying how much you love him as he goes to sleep. There will be no fear, and the last thing your dog will remember is your love.

Grieving   A well-loved dog is an emotional investment of unparalleled returns. Unfortunately, our dogs' lives are entirely too short and we must learn to cope with inevitably losing them. Grief is a natural reaction to the loss of a loved one, whether it is a pet, a spouse, friend or family member. Grief has no set pattern; its intensity and duration are different for each person and for each loss.

Sometimes the best outlet for grief is a good hard cry. For others, talking about their pet is good therapy. It's especially helpful to talk to people who've also lost an old dog and can relate to your loss. You may want to bury your old friend in a special spot where you can go to remember the wonderful times you shared together. You could also ask your veterinarian about having your dog cremated and keeping his or her ashes in a special urn in your home.

Your Happy Healthy Pet

Your Dog's Name _____

Name on Your Dog's Pedigree (if your dog has one) _____

_____

Where Your Dog Came From _____

_____

Your Dog's Birthday _____

Your Dog's Veterinarian

    Name _____

    Address _____

    Phone Number_____

    Emergency Number_____

Your Dog's Health

    Vaccines

    type _____ date given _____

    type _____ date given _____

    type _____ date given _____

    type _____ date given _____

    Heartworm

    date tested _____ type used_____ start date _____

Your Dog's License Number_____

Groomer's Name and Number _____

Dogsitter/Walker's Name and Number_____

Awards Your Dog Has Won

    Award _____ date earned _____

    Award _____ date earned _____

part four

Beyond
the
Basics

Recommended Reading

Books

ABOUT HEALTH CARE

Ackerman, Lowell. *Guide to Skin and Haircoat Problems in Dogs.* Loveland, Colo.: Alpine Publications, 1994.

Alderton, David. *The Dog Care Manual.* Hauppauge, N.Y.: Barron's Educational Series, Inc., 1986.

American Kennel Club. *American Kennel Club Dog Care and Training.* New York: Howell Book House, 1991.

Bamberger, Michelle, DVM. *Help! The Quick Guide to First Aid for Your Dog.* New York: Howell Book House, 1995.

Carlson, Delbert, DVM, and James Giffin, MD. *Dog Owner's Home Veterinary Handbook.* New York: Howell Book House, 1992.

DeBitetto, James, DVM, and Sarah Hodgson. *You & Your Puppy.* New York: Howell Book House, 1995.

Humphries, Jim, DVM. *Dr. Jim's Animal Clinic for Dogs.* New York: Howell Book House, 1994.

McGinnis, Terri. *The Well Dog Book.* New York: Random House, 1991.

Pitcairn, Richard and Susan. *Natural Health for Dogs.* Emmaus, Pa.: Rodale Press, 1982.

ABOUT DOG SHOWS

Hall, Lynn. *Dog Showing for Beginners.* New York: Howell Book House, 1994.

Nichols, Virginia Tuck. *How to Show Your Own Dog.* Neptune, N. J.: TFH, 1970.

Vanacore, Connie. *Dog Showing, An Owner's Guide.* New York: Howell Book House, 1990.

ABOUT TRAINING

Ammen, Amy. *Training in No Time.* New York: Howell Book House, 1995.

Baer, Ted. *Communicating With Your Dog.* Hauppauge, N.Y.: Barron's Educational Series, Inc., 1989.

Benjamin, Carol Lea. *Dog Problems.* New York: Howell Book House, 1989.

Benjamin, Carol Lea. *Dog Training for Kids.* New York: Howell Book House, 1988.

Benjamin, Carol Lea. *Mother Knows Best.* New York: Howell Book House, 1985.

Benjamin, Carol Lea. *Surviving Your Dog's Adolescence.* New York: Howell Book House, 1993.

Bohnenkamp, Gwen. *Manners for the Modern Dog.* San Francisco: Perfect Paws, 1990.

Dibra, Bashkim. *Dog Training by Bash.* New York: Dell, 1992.

Dunbar, Ian, PhD, MRCVS. *Dr. Dunbar's Good Little Dog Book,* James & Kenneth Publishers, 2140 Shattuck Ave. #2406, Berkeley, Calif. 94704. (510) 658–8588. Order from the publisher.

Dunbar, Ian, PhD, MRCVS. *How to Teach a New Dog Old Tricks,* James & Kenneth Publishers. Order from the publisher; address above.

Dunbar, Ian, PhD, MRCVS, and Gwen Bohnenkamp. Booklets on *Preventing Aggression; Housetraining; Chewing; Digging; Barking; Socialization; Fearfulness; and Fighting,* James & Kenneth Publishers. Order from the publisher; address above.

Evans, Job Michael. *People, Pooches and Problems.* New York: Howell Book House, 1991.

Kilcommons, Brian and Sarah Wilson. *Good Owners, Great Dogs.* New York: Warner Books, 1992.

McMains, Joel M. *Dog Logic—Companion Obedience.* New York: Howell Book House, 1992.

Rutherford, Clarice and David H. Neil, MRCVS. *How to Raise a Puppy You Can Live With.* Loveland, Colo.: Alpine Publications, 1982.

Volhard, Jack and Melissa Bartlett. *What All Good Dogs Should Know: The Sensible Way to Train.* New York: Howell Book House, 1991.

ABOUT BREEDING

Harris, Beth J. Finder. *Breeding a Litter, The Complete Book of Prenatal and Postnatal Care.* New York: Howell Book House, 1983.

Holst, Phyllis, DVM. *Canine Reproduction.* Loveland, Colo.: Alpine Publications, 1985.

Walkowicz, Chris and Bonnie Wilcox, DVM. *Successful Dog Breeding, The Complete Handbook of Canine Midwifery.* New York: Howell Book House, 1994.

ABOUT ACTIVITIES

American Rescue Dog Association. *Search and Rescue Dogs.* New York: Howell Book House, 1991.

Barwig, Susan and Stewart Hilliard. *Schutzhund.* New York: Howell Book House, 1991.

Beaman, Arthur S. *Lure Coursing.* New York: Howell Book House, 1994.

Daniels, Julie. *Enjoying Dog Agility—From Backyard to Competition.* New York: Doral Publishing, 1990.

Davis, Kathy Diamond. *Therapy Dogs.* New York: Howell Book House, 1992.

Gallup, Davis Anne. *Running With Man's Best Friend.* Loveland, Colo.: Alpine Publications, 1986.

Habgood, Dawn and Robert. *On the Road Again With Man's Best Friend.* New England, Mid-Atlantic, West Coast and Southeast editions. Selective guides to area bed and breakfasts, inns, hotels and resorts that welcome guests and their dogs. New York: Howell Book House, 1995.

Holland, Vergil S. *Herding Dogs.* New York: Howell Book House, 1994.

LaBelle, Charlene G. *Backpacking With Your Dog.* Loveland, Colo.: Alpine Publications, 1993.

Simmons-Moake, Jane. *Agility Training, The Fun Sport for All Dogs.* New York: Howell Book House, 1991.

Spencer, James B. *Hup! Training Flushing Spaniels the American Way.* New York: Howell Book House, 1992.

Spencer, James B. *Point! Training the All-Seasons Birddog.* New York: Howell Book House, 1995.

Tarrant, Bill. *Training the Hunting Retriever.* New York: Howell Book House, 1991.

Volhard, Jack and Wendy. *The Canine Good Citizen.* New York: Howell Book House, 1994.

General Titles

Haggerty, Captain Arthur J. *How to Get Your Pet Into Show Business.* New York: Howell Book House, 1994.

McLennan, Bardi. *Dogs and Kids, Parenting Tips.* New York: Howell Book House, 1993.

Moran, Patti J. *Pet Sitting for Profit, A Complete Manual for Professional Success.* New York: Howell Book House, 1992.

Scalisi, Danny and Libby Moses. *When Rover Just Won't Do, Over 2,000 Suggestions for Naming Your Dog*. New York: Howell Book House, 1993.

Sife, Wallace, PhD. *The Loss of a Pet*. New York: Howell Book House, 1993.

Wrede, Barbara J. *Civilizing Your Puppy*. Hauppauge, N.Y.: Barron's Educational Series, 1992.

Magazines

The AKC GAZETTE, The Official Journal for the Sport of Purebred Dogs. American Kennel Club, 51 Madison Ave., New York, NY.

Bloodlines Journal. United Kennel Club, 100 E. Kilgore Rd., Kalamazoo, MI.

Dog Fancy. Fancy Publications, 3 Burroughs, Irvine, CA 92718

Dog World. Maclean Hunter Publishing Corp., 29 N. Wacker Dr., Chicago, IL 60606.

Videos

"SIRIUS Puppy Training," by Ian Dunbar, PhD, MRCVS. James & Kenneth Publishers, 2140 Shattuck Ave. #2406, Berkeley, CA 94704. Order from the publisher.

"Training the Companion Dog," from Dr. Dunbar's British TV Series, James & Kenneth Publishers. (See address above).

The American Kennel Club produces videos on every breed of dog, as well as on hunting tests, field trials and other areas of interest to purebred dog owners. For more information, write to AKC/Video Fulfillment, 5580 Centerview Dr., Suite 200, Raleigh, NC 27606.

Resources

Breed Clubs

Every breed recognized by the American Kennel Club has a national (parent) club. National clubs are a great source of information on your breed. You can get the name of the secretary of the club by contacting:

The American Kennel Club
51 Madison Avenue
New York, NY 10010
(212) 696-8200

There are also numerous all-breed, individual breed, obedience, hunting and other special-interest dog clubs across the country. The American Kennel Club can provide you with a geographical list of clubs to find ones in your area. Contact them at the above address.

Registry Organizations

Registry organizations register purebred dogs. The American Kennel Club is the oldest and largest in this country, and currently recognizes over 130 breeds. The United Kennel Club registers some breeds the AKC doesn't (including the American Pit Bull Terrier and the Miniature Fox Terrier) as well as many of the same breeds. The others included here are for your reference; the AKC can provide you with a list of foreign registries.

American Kennel Club
51 Madison Avenue
New York, NY 10010

United Kennel Club (UKC)
100 E. Kilgore Road
Kalamazoo, MI 49001-5598

American Dog Breeders Assn.
P.O. Box 1771
Salt Lake City, UT 84110
(Registers American Pit Bull Terriers)

Canadian Kennel Club
89 Skyway Avenue
Etobicoke, Ontario
Canada M9W 6R4

National Stock Dog Registry
P.O. Box 402
Butler, IN 46721
(Registers working stock dogs)

Orthopedic Foundation for Animals (OFA)
2300 E. Nifong Blvd.
Columbia, MO 65201-3856
(Hip registry)

Activity Clubs

Write to these organizations for information on the
activities they sponsor.

American Kennel Club
51 Madison Avenue
New York, NY 10010
(Conformation Shows, Obedience Trials, Field
Trials and Hunting Tests, Agility, Canine Good

Citizen, Lure Coursing, Herding, Tracking,
Earthdog Tests, Coonhunting.)

United Kennel Club
100 E. Kilgore Road
Kalamazoo, MI 49001-5598
(Conformation Shows, Obedience Trials, Agility,
Hunting for Various Breeds, Terrier Trials and
more.)

North American Flyball Assn.
1342 Jeff St.
Ypsilanti, MI 48198

International Sled Dog Racing Assn.
P.O. Box 446
Norman, ID 83848-0446

North American Working Dog Assn., Inc.
Southeast Kreisgruppe
P.O. Box 833
Brunswick, GA 31521

Trainers

Association of Pet Dog Trainers
P.O. Box 3734
Salinas, CA 93912
(408) 663–9257

American Dog Trainers' Network
161 West 4th St.
New York, NY 10014
(212) 727–7257

**National Association of Dog Obedience
Instructors**
2286 East Steel Rd.
St. Johns, MI 48879

Associations

American Dog Owners Assn.
1654 Columbia Tpk.
Castleton, NY 12033
(Combats anti-dog legislation)

Delta Society
P.O. Box 1080
Renton, WA 98057-1080
(Promotes the human/animal bond through
pet-assisted therapy and other programs)

Dog Writers Assn. of America (DWAA)
Sally Cooper, Secy.
222 Woodchuck Ln.
Harwinton, CT 06791

National Assn. for Search and Rescue (NASAR)
P.O. Box 3709
Fairfax, VA 22038

Therapy Dogs International
1536 Morris Place
Hillside, NJ 07205